A WINDOW
TO CRITICISM

Shakespeare's *Sonnets* and
Modern Poetics

Thou art thy mother's glass, and she in thee
Calls back the lovely April of her prime.
So thou through windows of thine age shalt see,
Despite of wrinkles, this thy golden time.

A Window to Criticism

Shakespeare's *Sonnets* and Modern Poetics

BY MURRAY KRIEGER

PRINCETON, NEW JERSEY

PRINCETON UNIVERSITY PRESS

1964

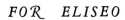

FOR ELISEO

PREFACE

I HAVE FELT a special challenge in writing this book. From the outset I have been deeply convinced of the essential unity of my subject. And I have realized that my most important task would be to persuade my readers that this unity was real and not specious, that this was not a yoking of heterogeneous elements, however disparate Shakespeare's *Sonnets* and modern poetics might appear to be. If I have earned my claim to the unity of my subject, through my use of the intervening and yet far-reaching metaphor of the mirror as window, then I can expect to have accomplished my other objectives, both theoretical and specifically related to the *Sonnets,* as well.

In the pages that follow, I must apologize for the number of occasions on which I find it necessary to refer to my own writings. I have tried to keep these references to a minimum; but, perhaps because of my innate single-mindedness, the more I work the more I find my various projects turning out to be aspects or developments of one project which I like to think of as a single body of theoretical and applied criticism. Consequently, I cannot help but feel the need to send the reader to reflections or further discussions of ideas in other places in earlier but related work.

Once again I should like to express my thanks to the John Simon Guggenheim Memorial Foundation, this time for the renewal of a fellowship that enabled me to undertake and complete this book. I am especially grateful to Gordon N. Ray for being as generous to me as Secretary-General of the Foundation as he was as my Provost at the University of Illinois. Of equal help in the completion of this project was an appointment as Associate Member at the Center for Advanced Study of the University of Illinois. I am thankful to the Center and to Frederick Wall, Dean of the Graduate College.

Many others, individuals and groups, have contributed to

what I have done here. Naomi Diamond of Wellesley College was an enthusiastic reader whose suggestions are directly reflected in this manuscript. John Hicks of *The Massachusetts Review* improved those portions of the book that appeared as an essay, "After the New Criticism," in that magazine. (These portions are reprinted here with the permission of the *Review*.) I have delivered portions of this book as lectures at the First Conference in Contemporary Literature at Michigan State University, at the Comparative Literature Conference of Harvard University, and at English Department groups of Brown University, Brandeis University, and the University of Massachusetts. For the provocative and suggestive reactions of these audiences I am grateful. But more helpful than all these was a small, hard-to-convince band of superior graduate students at the University of Illinois who, some years back, challenged me through an advanced seminar in critical theory that was continually exciting and stimulating to me, and forced me to crystallize my thinking in many areas where it had been helplessly vague.

The greatest individual contribution, however, was made by my good friend, Morton W. Bloomfield of Harvard University. Throughout my year's leave in 1961–1962, his endless patience, continual interest, and broad learning as both discussant and reader of my growing manuscript made their impress throughout this work and deepened it wherever they touched it. For his time and his warm intelligence I am grateful beyond words.

I call attention also to the indebtedness which I try in a small way to acknowledge in my dedication. It is one which I have acknowledged in my earlier writings but for which I can never hope to suggest a measurement. Finally, let me add one more word of my profound thankfulness to my wife, Joan, for patience, kindness, and—more specifically—for ideas and criticism. Neither the *Sonnets* nor modern poetics could have been nearly what they are for me and for this book without her help.

M. K.

Santuit Pond, Massachusetts
August 1963

CONTENTS

Preface   vii

I. The Mirror as Window in Recent
     Literary Theory   1

   1. The Resort to "Miracle" in Recent
      Poetics   3

   2. Contextualism and Its Alternatives   28

II. The Mirror as Window in Shakespeare's
     Sonnets   71

   Introductory   73

   1. The Mirror of Narcissus and the
      Magical Mirror of Love   80

   2. Truth vs. Troth: The Worms of the
      Vile, Wise World   118

   3. State, Property, and the Politics
      of Reason   140

   4. The Miracle of Love's Eschatology
      and Incarnation   165

III. The Power of Poetic Effigy   191

Index   219

Index of Sonnets   223

I

THE MIRROR

AS WINDOW IN RECENT

LITERARY THEORY

1. THE RESORT TO "MIRACLE"
IN RECENT POETICS

THIS BOOK intends to move beyond the New Criticism. If I were bolder, I would call it "Through the Looking Glass." I would mean the title literally; indeed, it would probably be more precisely accurate than the one I am using. In the light of recent literary criticism and aesthetics, let me so oversimplify questions about the language of poems[1] as to say categorically that there are essentially three ways in which we can view this language as functioning: (1) as window to the world, (2) as an enclosed set of endlessly faceted mirrors ever multiplying its maze of reflections but finally shut up within itself, and (3) as this same set of mirrors that miraculously becomes window again after all. Of these alternatives much more later. I merely comment in a general way here that to see the language of poems functioning as window, with meaning coming *through* it, was the way of the pre-New Criticism still all too much with us; to see it as the set of mirrors, with meaning locked *in* it, was commonly the way of the New Criticism in its most distinctive and instructive, if most limited, forms; but to see it the third way—to see the mirrors as window too, to see the poem as both trapping us *in* the looking glass and taking us *through* it—this is to move beyond the New Criticism, to get through the poem's closed context back to history and existence in a way which I hope criticism will increasingly be doing.[2] I mean in this book to

---

[1] I use "poems" here instead of "poetry" to emphasize that I mean to talk about discrete works and not, like Northrop Frye, about the body of all poetry as if it constituted a single entity.

[2] It should be evident even at this early stage that my use of the metaphor of the mirror in my opposition between the mirror and the window functions of language is in no way like that of M. H. Abrams in his well-known opposition between the mirror and the lamp (*The Mirror and the Lamp: Romantic Theory and the Critical Tradition*, New

3

furnish a theoretical justification for its doing so, to construct a new bridge that would connect the insular criticism of literature as literature with the mainland of man's concerns as a social-historical being.

[i]

For many recent critics, the problem of metaphor is a microcosm of the problem of poetry, a reduction of the problem to extremely precise and manageable form. For these critics the definition of poetry, in distinction to rhetoric or pseudo-rhetoric, is an enlargement of the definition of functional metaphor, in distinction to decorative analogy. This may also be an oversimplification, but it is a useful one with which to begin our explorations.

The most exciting discussions of metaphor by recent critics, in their desperate attempts finally to explain its mysterious workings and powers, have invariably ended by invoking the miraculous. The form of miracle is one either vaguely or

---

York, 1953). This is to say that mine is in no way like the metaphor of the mirror as it has been used in the long critical tradition—indeed from Plato onward—as the governing metaphor in mimetic theory. As Abrams makes so helpfully clear, the epistemology behind the conventional use of mirror to describe the mimetic function of art asserts the possible (and desirable) equation between external reality and the reality that is created within the symbols of art, so that the latter mirrors the former. This of course is to assert that language can (and should) be used as faithful mirror of reality. A slight shift of metaphor would allow us to see it, from the other side, as a transparent, unrefracting window upon reality. In this sense, the conventional mirror serves in a way that in this opening statement I have been assigning to the window. And so it is with what, following Spenser, I shall later term the "glass of crystal clean" (see Part II, Section 1, below). For I have reserved a more spectacular function for my rather special mirror and its remarkable powers. Instead of being a simple matter of giving back the reality it faces—even as, with a window, we can see through to reality—mine is a set of mirrors that is closed to external reality but that reflects within and among its members in a series of multiple angles of illusion. Instead of facing external reality, then, my mirror turns its back on the outside world.

4

precisely analogous to the Incarnation, the word made body. The reason for this resort to miracle is plain, I believe, once we see it in light of the implied criteria for metaphor that seem to underlie these discussions.

Influenced as these critics are by "metaphysical" techniques, they require at once logical precision and the unpredictable shock. They begin by demanding, on the lowest level, consistency within the terms of the "vehicle" of the metaphor. Secondly, the metaphor is to exhibit what Allen Tate termed "tension" in the relation of its "vehicle" to its "tenor." That is, the reader should be able to trace an unbroken series of connections or translations from its most extravagant reaches back to its homely and literal beginnings. The metaphoric extensions are to exhibit nothing of incoherence or discontinuity about them to the careful reader, as level empties into level.[3] However, although the sensible, hardheaded obligations of metaphor are exhausted in these first two criteria, we are still left at the outermost, if most intellectually artful, limits of decorative analogy, and only at the threshold of a poetry that has begun to breathe on its own. To enter it, there is a third and more mystic demand to be met, as mystic as the very daring at the bottom of organic and contextualist thinking about poetry. Although the first two criteria would seem to preclude the possibility of any leap, of any logical discontinuity, yet there is at last to be a leap of meaning, a final and original twist that reveals a new relation—unperceived and unpredictable before now—found in the terms of the vehicle that could not have been seen within the confines of the tenor by itself. This relation, that is uncovered in the

[3] Allen Tate, *On the Limits of Poetry* (New York, 1948), pp. 75–90, especially pp. 82–83. Elsewhere, describing the "Symbolic Imagination," a term he invented later which seems to be a thematic equivalent of the more technical device of "tension," Tate says similarly, ". . . it sees not only with but through the natural world. . . . It never begins at the top; it carries the bottom along with it, however high it may climb." *The Man of Letters in the Modern World* (New York, 1955), p. 112.

vehicle, now enriches the tenor in its reflection, even if we cannot merely re-translate it back. For it is totally *in*, and not merely *through*, the relations within the vehicle that this new relation can now be perceived. Somehow the vehicle has carried us, step by traceable step, to what startles us in its relevance, its inevitability, and yet its *logical* untraceability— unless, using language perhaps too loosely, we wish to allow the metaphor its own baffling "logic," a parody of our own logic that once seemed to rule the metaphor only to have been at last overruled by it.[4] This third criterion requires us to see the vehicle functioning as window for the tenor even as it is its own mirror trapping us within its internalized reflections. It is here that the poem becomes substance as well as empty sign, that it takes on the life that makes it unique and irreplaceable.

This view of metaphor is the ground for an entire poetics and for the organicism and contextualism that characterize it. Paradox lies at the very heart of it, calling for miraculous resolution—miraculous at least in relation to our commonsense notions of the distinctions between mere terms and actual things, between rational coherence and inexplicable emergence. For this literary theory is moved primarily by the need to see poetry as breaking through the seemingly inevitable dualism in our normal sense of language, to make poetry into that magically monistic effigy that is not merely an empty sign through which we are directed to things, but rather both the sign and the substantive thing itself. As in the mystic approach to the Old Testament God, all must be found in the word, as word and thing—indeed word and world—are made one. Poetry as the word is no longer, like

[4] This paradoxical claim that the miracle, though miracle, must somehow be earned reflects the attempt of these would-be neoclassical critics to provide a hardheaded alternative to the romantic poet's leap from image to idea, from real to ideal. They want the miracle but do not want to come to it through the speciously poetic means that Yvor Winters aptly termed "pseudo-reference."

6

other uses of language, burdened with a simple about-ness, so that it may be more troublesomely burdened with its own expansive embodiment of the substance that is the world.

Thus John Crowe Ransom, out of a desire to cherish rather than to use the world, struggles to escape from the need to choose between two unsatisfying alternatives—a "pure," unelevated poetry about things (as in imagism) and an abstract, Platonic poetry about ideas—by calling for a poetry of "miraculism" that is somehow neither and both. Insisting, in words that remind us of Tate's later definition of "tension," that "the miracle must have a basis of verisimilitude," Ransom sees miraculism "when the poet discovers by analogy an identity between objects which is partial, though it should be considerable, and proceeds to an identification which is complete."[5] He continues, "It is to be contrasted with the simile, which says 'as if' or 'like,' and is scrupulous to keep the identification partial." Of course, partial "identification" or "identity" (and in either case I would prefer to say "similarity" to distinguish it from identity, which seems to me to involve totality) implies partial difference as well and thus a firm distinction between the two, the tenor and vehicle. The fundamental law of logic is of course the law of identity, which is to keep us from confusing distinct entities, to keep them from overrunning the bounds of their distinctness. The miracle, then, arises as the poet, through what seems merely to be "the extension of a rhetorical device," proclaims an absolute identity between them, in effect forces through a substantive transfer of properties. It follows for Ransom to say "that the miraculism which produces the humblest conceit is the same miraculism which supplies to religions their substantive content." It would for him be as much an incarnating act, as much a defiance of our dull world of logic, for Donne, in *The Canonization*, to make us—within the context of the

[5] "Poetry: a Note in Ontology," *The World's Body* (New York, 1938), pp. 139–140, for these quotations and those which follow.

poem—accept his lovers literally and not just figuratively as saints (totally *as* saints and not just in part like and in part unlike them) as it is for the religious experience to make its enthusiast see the wine *as* blood and not just as a surrogate sharing *some* of the properties of blood.

This terminology is more applicable to Allen Tate, who uses the theological analogue more centrally. It is most apparent in his later work as a Catholic, specifically in his brilliant twin essays on "The Symbolic Imagination" and "The Angelic Imagination" (1951). But we find earlier evidence of this tendency, as early as "Three Types of Poetry" (1934), where, as in the later essay on "The Symbolic Imagination," Dante creates the need for him to break through the seeming dualism of allegory to the dynamic monism of poetry's expressive fullness. We find everywhere the same antagonism to semantic dualism in poetry, to a poetry "about" ideas, as we saw in Ransom, who liked to think of this antagonism as a healthy anti-Platonism. In the earlier essay, Tate treats what we usually think of as allegory quite harshly ("inferior as science . . . inferior as poetry"[6]) but exempts from his charges a special, if archaic, kind of allegory, Dante's "religious allegory." This kind "is both literally and figuratively true: we are to believe that the events of the story happened. But poetical allegory is true only in the figurative sense. . . . [It leans] upon no basis of fact." Thus poetical allegory, like the Platonism detested by Ransom, scorns its beginnings in the stuff of experience, its "basis of verisimilitude," so that it can hardly be a candidate for Tate's "tension." But, Tate continues, "When the medieval allegorist used the Bible, it never entered his head that he was not using historical fact." Where supposed fact and mythological construct are one, supposed fact can take an aesthetic form and have spiritual

[6] This quotation and others which follow from "Three Types of Poetry" are from *On the Limits of Poetry* (New York, 1948), pp. 95–96.

8

consequences without having to cease being the supposed fact. Here we can more easily satisfy the continuity demanded by "tension." Consequently, "although *The Divine Comedy* is allegorical, it would not be one of the great poems of all time if Dante had not believed its structure to be true. It came out of an age whose mentality held the allegorical view of experience as easily as we hold the causal and scientific; so, in Dante, allegory never rises to an insubordinate place, but consistently occupies an implicit place, from which we must derive it by analysis."

In his essay almost two decades later, Tate tries to "derive it" in just this way, and his formulations indicate a consistency with his earlier probing essay that suggests his conversion to Catholicism did not make so radical a change in his critical work as some have suggested, but rather sharpened the precision of his earlier notions and furnished a most helpful analogical vocabulary to describe the "Unitive Way" of poetry.[7] Always, as in his earlier claims for "tension" and in Ransom's claims for an anti-Platonic "miraculism," the most transcendent reaches of Dante's metaphors remain responsive to the common reality out of which they issue. Again and again there is an accumulation of levels, the top of which manages to "include," rather than to "reject" the bottom and the most literal and commonplace of them (pp. 94 and 112, among others). Thus "three dancing girls appear: Dante's allegory, formidable as it is, intensifies rather than impoverishes the reality of the dancers as girls. Their dance is a real dance, their song . . . is a real song" (p. 94). Tate approvingly quotes Charles Williams: "It was, however high the phrases, the common thing from which Dante always started, as it was certainly the greatest and most common to which he came" (p. 97). The phrase, "the common thing,"

---

[7] "The Symbolic Imagination," *The Man of Letters in the Modern World* (New York, 1955), p. 102. Further quotations from this essay (pp. 93–112) will be followed by their page references in parentheses.

becomes a central one for Tate in his celebration of Dante's devotion to it. He speaks even of "the return of the supra-rational and supra-sensible to the 'common thing' " (p. 102) in proclaiming the extent to which Dante is "committed to the visible." And a bit later: "He not only begins with the common thing; he continues with it, until at the end we come by disarming stages to a scene that no man has ever looked upon before. Every detail of Paradise is a common thing; it is the cumulative combination and recombination of natural objects beyond their 'natural' relations, which staggers the imagination" (p. 110).

Tate also generalizes about the operation of the symbolic imagination, as distinguished from the "angelic imagination" which, with an anti-Platonism that reminds us of Ransom, he sees as the unhappy result of the intellect's attempt to bypass the world of the senses to gain "direct knowledge of essences." Hence the "angelic imagination" is that which means pre-sumptuously to transcend "the mediation of both image and discourse," which "tries to disintegrate or to circumvent the image in the illusory pursuit of essence" (p. 97). The true poet knows better: "Despite the timeless orders of both ra-tional discourse and intuitive contemplation, it is the business of the symbolic poet to return to the order of temporal se-quence—to *action*. His purpose is to show men experiencing whatever they may be capable of, with as much meaning as he may be able to see in it; but the action comes first. Shall we call this the Poetic Way? It is at any rate the way of the poet, who has got to do his work with the body of this world . . ." (p. 96). It is this "Poetic" and "symbolic" way of the imagination that enables Tate to speak of its work as "proximate incarnations of the Word" (p. 99), "shocking" in the fused simultaneity that crowns and transforms the step-by-step metaphorical climb from the "common thing" which is somehow still there at the end. Here indeed is an extension of Ransom's "miraculism" and its relation to the "substantive content" of religions.

Dante similarly inspires Erich Auerbach, moving him to a most powerful typological reading of the medieval literary "realism" of *The Divine Comedy*. Again it is the substantive union of distinct entities that his "figural interpretation" depends on,[8] and it is in Dante that he finds its most brilliant manifestation. The *"figura"* has a double reality, its own historical reality within linear time and a meta-historical reality partaking of the ultimate appearance of the timeless in time, an appearance which the *figura* anticipates. The anticipation by the *figura* is answered by the "fulfillment," which confirms that anticipation and its role in the divine scheme. Thus "an occurrence on earth signifies not only itself but at the same time another, which it predicts or confirms, without prejudice to the power of its concrete reality here and now" (p. 555). The transcendent prepares the phenomenal world of history for the appearance of the divine within its realm by creating foreshadowings of the ultimate, "fulfilling" appearance among those discrete personages who carry on the drama of history. History is transformed to typology, its dramas at once immediate or self-determined and ultimate or metaphysically determined. All is absorbed to the single grand scheme everywhere reverberating, but somehow all retains a differentiating selfhood too. History and mythology attain the mysterious union which Tate also admires for the substantive oneness it allowed to poetry. The consequences upon the substance of reality—Tate's "common thing"—and upon the substance of language should be clear: "a figural schema per-

---

[8] *Mimesis: The Representation of Reality in Western Literature*, trans. Willard R. Trask (Princeton, 1953), pp. 194–202, for his typological reading of Dante. Among other passages dealing with "figural interpretation," see especially pp. 48, 73–76, 156–162, 247–248, and 555.

mits both its poles—the figure and its fulfillment—to retain
the characteristics of concrete historical reality, in contradis-
tinction to what obtains with symbolic or allegorical person-
ifications, so that figure and fulfillment—although the one
signifies the other—have a significance which is not incompatible with their being real. An event taken as a figure
preserves its literal and historical meaning. It remains an
event, does not become a mere sign" (pp. 195–196).

His view of Dante's "unitive" power must here join Tate's:
"This enables us to understand that the beyond is eternal and
yet phenomenal; that it is changeless and of all time and yet
full of history" (p. 197). Thus Dante can give us "an emotion which is concerned with human beings and not directly
with the divine order in which they have found their fulfillment. Their eternal position in the divine order is something
of which we are only conscious as a setting whose irrevocabil-
ity can but serve to heighten the effect of their humanity, preserved for us in all its force. The result is a direct experience
of life which overwhelms everything else . . ." (p. 201).
Auerbach can conclude on Dante as paradoxically as does
Tate, with an appeal to the miracle that can assert at once the
incompatible claims of the historical and the meta-historical
orders: "Dante's work made man's Christian-figural being a
reality, and destroyed it in the very process of realizing it"
(p. 202). Once more Ransom's "miraculism" in poetry is
extended to and defined by a religious mythology which makes
the mediate immediate and the apparent substantive, even as
they remain themselves.

Leo Spitzer refers to Auerbach's treatment of Dante as he
too uses this poet as his example of the substantive—as opposed to the merely allegorical—powers of poetry: "We may
remember that the capacity of giving the evidence of the
flesh and of temporal development to spiritual experience is
first found with the greatest medieval poet, Dante, who, in the
place of timeless allegories of the perfect Beloved, substituted

the graphic image of a Beatrice who actually walks, smiles, sighs, within a poem that has a beginning, a middle and an end . . . Modern lyricism, even of a wordly kind, is indebted to such religious poets as Dante and Juan de la Cruz for the evidence (evidence of the flesh and evidence of time) which they have given forever to the description of inner feeling."[9]

Elsewhere Spitzer speaks explicitly of the miraculous nature of these powers and attributes them to metaphysical wit in a way that reminds us of Ransom: "Wit, which here, as always with Marvell, has a functional role, suggests the possibility of a miracle: the possibility of moral or spiritual qualities becoming sensuously perceptible as though they were objects in outward nature. . . . A miracle is after all nothing but the substantiation of the supernatural."[10]

Again like Ransom, he relates the poet's miracle to the religious miracle without equating them: "This is, of course, a miracle of the poet's making, but one that goes back historically to medieval religious beliefs, according to which the spirituality of saints and martyrs acted in similar analogy on the physical world. Metaphysical wit has here simply laicized, and preserved in poetry, the substantiation of the supernatural current in hagiographic legend. . . . Some of this quasi-religious comic spirit or awesome wit (poetry being, as is so often the case, the re-enactment in secularized form of ancestral beliefs) is also present in Marvell's suggestion that the animal

[9] "Three Poems on Ecstasy (John Donne, St. John of the Cross, Richard Wagner)," *Essays on English and American Literature*, by Leo Spitzer, ed. Anna Hatcher (Princeton, 1962), p. 171.
[10] "Marvell's 'Nymph Complaining for the Death of Her Fawn': Sources versus Meaning," *Essays on English and American Literature*, p. 107. In a footnote to this passage Spitzer clearly divorces the miracle from any necessary connection with the supernatural so as to make it a poetic device: "On the contrary, 'poetic miracles' performed by a Marino have, it seems to me, no supernatural connotations: with him the transformation is from one sensuous object to another, more perfect in its sensuous beauty." He goes on to discuss a passage controlled by the "alchemy" that produces "an entirely sensuous miracle."

lying among lilies and feeding on roses may become all lilies and roses. Here the poetic miracle has inherited from the truly religious miracle its paradoxical logic, its psycho-physical analogy, and the mechanization of the spiritual (there is no 'cynicism' involved in such a transfer)." (pp. 109–110)

A very exciting younger critic, Sigurd Burckhardt, has at the center of his approach a claim close to this notion of poetry's peculiarly substantive nature. He sees poems, through their manipulation of metaphor, phonetic relations, double meanings, as taking on what he terms "corporeality"—clearly much the same sort of thing as incarnation—as the poetic word itself becomes the entity, the holder, and not just the transmitter, of power.[11] The poet is to "release words in some measure from their bondage to meaning, their purely referential role, and to give or restore to them the corporeality which a true medium needs." He must, in other words, take from language the handicap it has in contrast to the physical media of the plastic arts. As they operate in culture, words come with ready-made meanings that inhibit the poet who would form them with the freedom the sculptor can use upon the unformed stuff with which he works. If I may introduce my own analogy to extend this valuable insight, the ready-made referentiality of language makes it more difficult for the poet to keep the reader from—in effect—eating the oranges off his work of art than it is for the still-life painter, whose physical medium is obviously unusable and insignificant, except for what he does with it in his art. Thus, Burckhardt goes on, the poet must "drive a wedge between words and their meanings, lessen as much as possible their designatory force and thereby inhibit our all too ready flight from them to the things they point to." Thus the pun, for example, "is the creation of a semantic identity between words whose phonetic

[11] See especially his splendid essay, "The Poet as Fool and Priest," *ELH*, XXIII (1956), 279–298. For the present discussion see pp. 279–287 of the essay.

14

identity is, for ordinary language, the merest coincidence. That is to say, it is an act of verbal violence, designed to tear the close bond between a word and its meaning. It asserts that mere phonetic—i.e. material, corporeal—likeness establishes likeness of meaning." With devices like this, the poet must work to give "the word as entity primacy over the word as sign."

It is in much the same sense that I have said elsewhere that the poet "damages language [that is, language in its normal relations] to show how much it can do," that he "does violence to language in order to celebrate language," thereby revealing the "comparative poverty" and "the inherent incapacities of all nonpoetic uses of language."[12] Viewed in this light, Burckhardt is doing more than quibbling when he maintains, in speaking of ambiguity in poetry, that it is not so important to see—as Empson does—that one word can "have *many meanings*" as it is to see "that many meanings can have *one word*." Again and again we shall see the applicability of this notion of "corporeality" when we come to examine Shakespeare's *Sonnets*. For the present purpose, the most immediate and brilliantly obvious example I would use to illustrate at a glance the claim of incarnation *in* the word occurs in the lines from Donne's *A Valediction Forbidding Mourning*,

> Dull sublunary lovers' love,
> Whose soul is sense, cannot admit
> Absence, because it doth remove
> Those things that elemented it.

Here, with a pun on "absence" that covers a winking etymology, "sense" is forced upon us as the root of "ab*sence*" in letter as well as concept. We are taught what "absence" really is: a word with a soul of "sense," with "sense" the

---

[12] *The New Apologists for Poetry* (Minneapolis, 1956), p. 75.

15

thing "that elemented it" and thus the thing that "cannot admit" it since "absence" involves—in word and concept, in word *as* concept—the deprivation, indeed the elimination of "sense." Donne's case is poetically "proved," for, as Burckhardt would claim the poet must, Donne has created a unique philology where all is teleological and there are no accidents. Surely we cannot place this operation of language within the proper bounds of ordinary discourse which ought to know better to keep its place and not make itself into things.

[ii]

Of course, the magically monistic "body" of a literary work is most demonstrable in verse, with its infinite capacities for manipulation of reference-breaking devices that depend on and are inseparable from its phonetic and linguistic form. Thus the overwhelming predominance of poems in the narrow sense (as opposed to the broad Aristotelian sense which would include more than verse) as the objects under criticism by writers in this theoretical tradition. However, if these claims are to have any theoretical force for general poetics, they would have to be applicable to fiction and drama, especially nonpoetic drama, these being media which cannot be as dependent on the unique, untranslatable word. Yet they too must rest on the sort of miracle we have seen postulated about metaphor and other devices of verse: on the claim that in the literary work discourse can be made into a substantive body. Though it is far more difficult to demonstrate this claim as the work increases in length and lets up on its verbal tightness and on the disciplined control of its strategies, other aspects can be examined to find ways in which it too cuts itself off to make itself whole. Yet undeniably there seems to be an obviously nagging referentiality to imaginative literature in prose which often seems to ally it more to ordinary discourse than to verse. And, admittedly, most works in prose *are* more mixed and impure in their nature, more sporadic in

16

the efficacy with which they perform their miracles. Still, the claim for a poetics of incarnation in the word must undertake to show that the novel or play should also be a self-sufficient entity that somehow closes itself off from normal discursive duality to become body, at once the source and the mouth of meaning.

Since my energies here are to be severely limited to verse— and to that small and tightly controlled form of verse, the sonnet—this book is not the place to argue the extension of this theory to prose forms of what, more broadly speaking, we would with Aristotle term "poetry." I have argued these extensions in detail elsewhere and will be doing so again.[13] But I believe it is worth digressing briefly here to indicate the one underlying way in which the body-producing miracle may be invoked prior to the special and unrestricted "iconic" techniques of verse, since this way may point to a more broadly useful poetics.

In my claims about the tragic vision, we can find the assumption of three propositions which may be seen as more generalized versions of those about the window-functions and mirror-functions of language with which I began: (1) The literary work, in proportion to its value as literary work, reveals the full existential density of life as lived in all its desperate, unresolvable tensions; the unbridgeable oppositions that our philosophy must override and our daily living ignore for these to operate. Therefore literature is justified by re-

[13] My book *The Tragic Vision: Variations on a Theme in Literary Interpretation* (New York, 1960) is meant to be related to this theory (see especially p. ix and pp. 229–257); and I would hope that my treatment of novels there indicates ways in which the verbal medium— its formation of plot, character, and symbol and its undercutting of would-be propositions—can function as an enclosing agent outside the disciplines of verse. Thus my invention of "thematics" as a *literary* method—to be distinguished from the philosophic extraction of themes —designed to find existential equivalents of aesthetic configurations. The work which I shall be completing next, *The Classic Vision*, is intended to produce similar evidence in nontragic works.

lating itself directly to the world of experience. (2) The literary work, in proportion to its value as literary work, is a self-sufficient aesthetic system of intramural relations among symbols that together strive toward a oneness that contains its reader by compelling upon him a unified response that inhibits an escape to the world. Therefore literature is justified by creating itself as a separate, self-sustaining world of terminal values. But these two propositions seem mutually contradictory, the second sealing literature off from extramural life and the first pointing it outward. Thus (3) the literary work, in proportion to its value as literary work, is able miraculously to satisfy both propositions at once, being at once totally thematic and totally aesthetic, answerable to itself only by being answerable to the outside world.

All I found about tragedy and the tragic vision, both in the most important documents that defined them and in the novels themselves, ended with the union of these mutually denying dimensions, the formal or aesthetic and the existential or thematic. In Aristotle, in Hegel, in Nietzsche—though of course with enormously varying emphases—there is the formal satisfaction of a world that has come round, fulfilled and even bettered all expectations and made terms with itself, together with that raw edge of suffering, that breach in order revealed through the daring separateness of extremity. These are the aesthetic and the anti-aesthetic motives of literature, that which will have the order of a wholeness that secures its own system and that which will yield to the chaotic principles of opposition that existentially confront the "tragic visionary." Thus the dénouement and the catharsis, as what has been aroused through complication is purged and resettled in the unravelling; but always coupled with the lingering ache for horrors that have been and may be again, the awareness of which outlasts the satisfactions of the aesthetic illusion that has so masterfully controlled them. The problem of Oedipus is not philosophically "solved": does the aesthetic transcendence of him which we have witnessed leave us thematically at ease?

This, then, is the double mask of tragedy: the vision of chaos at the bottom of the moral order, which is to say the vision of no moral order, the heretical or Manichaean vision;[14] and that which converts it to art by creating the work that is a testament to order, the work that unifies it, transcends it, and in so doing tames it. The nightmare reality out of the underground depths in us all creates the destructive, anti-aesthetic motive that is intimately—too intimately—related to our experience in its darkness. And the refinement, the lightening, of our vision in an order that has been earned through crisis creates the aesthetic motive which provides, in its momentary purification, a token of wholeness in this microcosmic illusion.

The two motives, the aesthetic-formal and the thematic-existential, manifest themselves in the vision of the tragedy as a formal whole and the vision of the tragic visionary in his action and its consequences—*Oedipus the King* as the play and Oedipus as king and protagonist. The former contains and transcends the latter without blotting out his visionary meaning. We are reconciled to him even as his vision remains as unbearable as his fate. That the unbearable is borne, the un-

[14] The Manichaean implications of contextualist literary theory are clear enough and have been noted on several occasions. But, since there have been misunderstandings, I should emphasize here, as I do in *The Tragic Vision* (pp. 238–268) that there is really no *metaphysical* commitment to Manichaeism in the position. It derives from literary works and a critical method adequate to them, not from a philosophic analysis of the nature of reality. Inasmuch as it is concerned with fictions, which deal only with the dramatic—the phenomenological—level of existence, this critical approach, in its persistent concern with tensions, can suggest no more than an *apparent* Manichaeism, a Manichaean *face* of reality. This suggestion would not speak at all to the ontological question about the ultimate nature of reality. However, while it makes no cosmic denials, one could infer from it that, if there should be a rational ontological structure of reality, it does not get reflected onto the chaotic existential level.

reconcilable reconciled, is tragedy's miracle: the presence at once of unresolvable tensions among opposites and of the release and ease of catharsis.

In modern literature the form of the problem may change somewhat, since ours may be seen to be an excessively Dionysian literature that ends in tensions rather than in catharsis. If this is true, then the aesthetic-formal motive is being neglected for the cultivation of the thematic-existential. For irresolution or tension (using this word in its usual sense rather than in Tate's special sense) is at the heart of the anti-aesthetic Manichaean motive in its divisive frustration of the harmony of wholeness. It represents the subversive tendencies in the tragic vision which perhaps led Plato to outlaw tragedy and led Aristotle to answer Plato by basing his defense of it on the purgation of these very tendencies, leading to the greater health of society. But to the extent that the modern literary work succeeds as literary work, it too must win its struggle to be whole and thus must in its way subdue its tensions, at least provisionally, in accord with the demands of the aesthetic illusion. Through the totality of his work, the author must prove himself to be master of his most unbridled creature.

Finally we must ask: what is the relation of the aesthetic resolution of tension, necessary to produce the unified work of art, to any claim of a cosmic resolution of tension? the relation of aesthetic affirmation to thematic affirmation? Which is to ask: what is the relation of tension to the cathartic principle, the aesthetic expulsion and transcendence of tension? The answer that some recent novelists, in their desperation, have suggested may give us a clue to the larger answer. The point of view of the novel permits the use of a narrator, one who as fictive author creates the tragic visionary for us, lives vicariously through him, but in creating him as part of the work also keeps him in his place in the necessary scheme of a whole world. The narrator gives the visionary a voice as part of his own voice so that he may hear it apart from himself and learn to control it, even, if necessary, to allow it to be destroyed symbolically. Thus the purge may also be a self-purge for the narrator, like Ishmael's purge of the "damp, drizzly November" in his soul accomplished by the symbolic destruction of his creature Ahab that readies him for salvation by the Rachel. After all, Ishmael's narrative artistry has made Ahab into his creature. Still, the narrator does not answer, or furnish a true alternative to, the tragic visionary since he has not the daring to join him as agent. He can assimilate him aesthetically only because, in maintaining his aesthetic distance as consummate author he retreats from replacing him existentially. So the narrator cannot eliminate the tragic vision or "resolve" it thematically into a higher and harmonious truth that can guide action, but rather offers his total narrative as the containing form whose completeness can assert itself against even the chaotic force within it. He thrusts forth the work as the "body" that enforces its integral oneness even upon the subversive part that, as "the destructive element," would tear the body apart but that merely proves its greater mastery by the strain it places upon the aesthetic order, challenged but still dominant. The undestroyed body of the work, or at least the aesthetic illusion of its single presence, may serve as analogue—as guaranty—of that greater order, the bodied universe, that lies behind and even embraces all Manichaean challenges. It is like the paradox of hope in hopelessness that the narrator Zeitblom sees in Leverkühn's greatest work in Mann's *Doctor Faustus*, in which the tightly controlled expression of despair is a conquest of it, a discovery of the beyond-despair: as "the final despair achieves a voice," the fact that "a voice is given the creature for its woe" becomes an achievement that produces the "consolation" of the aesthetic paradox.[15]

This thrusting forth of the body of the work as the principle

[15] Thomas Mann, *Doctor Faustus*, trans. H. T. Lowe-Porter (New York, 1948), p. 491.

21

of containment and transcendence, though without any denial of the existential authenticity of what it aesthetically contains and transcends—what it has aesthetically mastered through expressing it within the confines of a work of art— is perhaps another version of the miracle of incarnation which we have seen the modern critique of metaphor assert. In drama or in prose fiction which makes less use of narrative techniques, the ways of imposing the body of the work as cosmos, as principle of order, are more varied and perhaps more difficult to perceive, though I would insist that in the great tragic work this imposition occurs, with the aesthetic and thematic consequences I have suggested. Plato and Aristotle are both right, the one in claiming the subversiveness of tragedy that calls for expulsion from the republic and the other in claiming the purgation, through the agency of the work itself, of the subversion to which it so violently and irrevocably exposes us. In tragedy we need the appeal to moral disorder even as we need the miracle of art that can turn even this most profound chaos into the order of art. The miracle may even persuade us that all chaos is finally somehow transcended and that aesthetic resolution *is* symbol of cosmic, that aesthetic affirmation *is* symbol of thematic-existential, that next time the moral dilemma can be evaded. But these are the deceptive reflections of the absoluteness of aesthetic illusion. For we must answer both "yes" and "no" when we ask whether we are really rid of the tension: we must be rid of it if we have the transcendent unity of the work of art that has succeeded, as cosmic body, in being one; but we cannot be rid of it if we have been convinced by the profound confrontation of absurdity we have witnessed.

We are back to the self-contradictory miracle of poetry in the broad sense. Here it is manifested by the simultaneous presence of the moral contradictions that create a tension of continual opposition, and of the soothing power of order that overcomes them, making them into an integral object. But the aesthetic illusion never quite shuts out the vision of reality as nightmare, never gives up the resistance, the existential courage, to insist that the tension has not been wished away. So in tragedy we have it and we don't have it; we drag the abyss and yet, as Nietzsche says, turn lamentation into a song of praise—though we never really rise very far. For we have not found answers that would satisfy the demands of everyday life or of moral philosophy. Instead every answer ultimately repeats the question once more.

Every commentator on tragedy must somewhere address the strange, obvious fact that we have an immense need for this witnessing of calamity, that the tragic pleasure is one that humanity can perhaps least forego. I believe it is the miracle I have cited—the conversion of tension to a catharsis which keeps it tension still—that accounts for the otherwise perverse pleasure we take in tragedy. I speak, of course, of the utter miracle that violates the law of contradiction in that it can be both itself and something else. It is what, for all its subversion, may render tragedy finally harmless even as it renders tragedy—in its anguish and grace, in its anguish *as* grace—a most indispensable art form.

I would maintain further that in our great nontragic literature too there is the awareness of the insoluble oppositions seen in any vision of life under the aspect of extremity. But in this literature there is a retreat from extremity, a withdrawal to the soundness and security of the solid center of living with its comforts and compromises that accompany its imposed or self-imposed blindness. But if the resources of life are welcome and are exploited richly, the fullness of this "classic vision" does not deny the extremity lurking just beyond the aesthetic frame, though it has been evaded—at a cost to the vision of the evading character. Even in many works of the highest comedy, extremity is there, if only by negation. Even here, then, I would maintain the miracle of an aesthetically asserted order held in the teeth of an unresolved tension that is not denied, though at moments it may come close to being wished away. Still it hovers teasingly, threateningly, on the fringe of the mature author's total vision, part of an awareness which dwarfs the awareness of his comic characters.

[iii]

Here, then, is a form of miracle analogous to that which we have seen recent critics urge in speaking of the deceptive dimensions of poetry in the narrower sense. Like the other, this miracle is dependent on the work's creating itself as body. As such, it should help me to argue generically for the incarnating capacities of any properly literary work. Indeed, the twin awareness of endlessly struggling tensions and of the miraculous body of the work which transcends them marks the conclusion by W. K. Wimsatt and Cleanth Brooks of their history of criticism, as they treat literature generically in terms of the higher resolutions of incarnation.[16] Thus they would generalize, as I would, upon the claims of those we examined earlier who were led to the invocation of this miracle. They reject for criticism "any of the Platonic or Gnostic ideal world views," echoing Ransom's rejection of Platonism and Tate's similar rejection of "the angelism of the intellect." In fact Gnosticism would seem to set the historical precedent for the presumptuous claim to the "angelic imagination" which Tate accuses modern man of making in his Cartesian arrogance. Consequently, poetry must not have the single voice that would reveal it to be enslaved to ideological meanings which deprive it of the fullness, what Burckhardt would call the "corporeality," it needs to achieve status as entity. But Wimsatt and Brooks reject at the other extreme

[16] *Literary Criticism: A Short History* (New York, 1957), p. 746. Wimsatt dwells at greater length on the conflict between tension and order in his "Poetic Tension: A Summary," *New Scholasticism,* XXXII (1958), 73–88.

"the Manichaean full dualism and strife of principles,"[17] which we have already seen as destructive of the order and harmony a work of art must attain. Between the Gnostic and Manichaean errors must be found the miraculous mean analogous to that of Christianity and as satisfying, if as difficult: "the vision of suffering, the optimism, the mystery which are embraced in the religious dogma of the Incarnation." And again the satisfaction, the seeming transcendence, arises out of the total, and totally meaningful, substantive "body" in whose grace the tensions are transformed as they are transfixed.

Philip Wheelwright comes by way of the anthropological study of primitive ritual to the fusion found in poetic language that has become a monistic effigy, at once pointer and substance of the thing pointed to. In this case the union in the word might seem to be "magical" rather than "miraculous," but it is the same phenomenon that is being described. Wheelwright sees it not only in all literature by virtue of its being "expressive" rather than "literal" discourse, but also in myth, ritual, and religion as other forms of this "expressive discourse." The logic and the semantic governing this discourse are governed by what, with the anthropologist Lévy-Bruhl, he describes as the "Law of Participation."[18] In the words of Lévy-Bruhl which he quotes, according to the workings of this law "objects and phenomena can be, though in a man-

---

[17] We must recognize at once that "dualism" here refers not to the thin "Platonic" referentiality in the relation between word and thing that I elsewhere speak of as the "dualistic use of language," but to the universal principle of ceaseless and absolute opposition of contradictory claims, both maintained at full and equal strength, as it characterizes the Manichaean vision. I try to make clear this distinction between the dualism or Platonism of language and the tensional dualism or Manichaeism of metaphysic (the latter being what Wimsatt and Brooks mean here) in *The Tragic Vision*, p. 241.

[18] *The Burning Fountain* (Bloomington, 1954), pp. 180–182, and the earlier discussion on p. 161.

ner incomprehensible to us, at once themselves and not themselves." For, as "pre-logical," the law "does not bind itself down, as logical thought does, to avoiding contradiction." Assertions of identity between entities both similar in some respects and dissimilar in others are to be taken as literal and absolute, however offensive such an assertion may be to our common-sense reason. And the imitation of life by art must not be seen as the insubstantial transparency of mere sign that points to a world of substance outside itself: as the "pre-logical" law has it, "a portrait . . . participates in the very nature, life and properties of the man whose image it is." Hence my use of the term "effigy" to characterize poetry in its capacity to function in this way.

Even Frazer, despite the elementary and superficial positivism that renders his anthropology obsolete, testifies continually to the substantive influx within the magical effigy, as an empowered image of either man or god.[19] He too relates this sort of monistic symbol, which gathers all within itself as at once image, substance, and act of meaning, to "the doctrine of transubstantiation" which allowed the primitives to eat "the very body of their god." Of course Frazer views with something between condescension and scorn the naive absurdity of this infant logic that confuses entities with one another by confusing signs with things they stand for. He is not ready, as Wheelwright is, to view his own common-sense notion of language and reality critically, to be open to the magical view that sees in existence a "fluidity" that "involves a flowing-into-one-another and disappearing-into-one-another of distinctions that to our way of looking at the matter are clear and definite" (*The Burning Fountain*, p. 161). This possibility stems from "an indefinable coalescence" between entities that allows the Navaho to sense the clouds, and with

---

[19] *The Golden Bough,* abr. ed. (New York, 1942), especially pp. 488–499. Of the several other discussions see also, for example, pp. 12–13, 650.

them the rain, literally within the puff of his tobacco-pipe smoke. Our capacity to entertain this vision allows us to enlarge our awareness of what poetry as this special kind of language can do, as my examination of Ransom, Tate, Auerbach, Spitzer, Burckhardt, Wimsatt and Brooks should have demonstrated and as my reading of Shakespeare's *Sonnets* is in part intended to demonstrate.

2. *CONTEXTUALISM AND ITS*
ALTERNATIVES

[i]

DESPITE the constant recurrence of religious terminology, the critics I have been discussing are trying not to theologize the act of poetry so much as to account for the way in which their experience has insisted that great poems work upon them and their most sensitive colleagues. What they say may sound like religious mysticism, although a writer like Spitzer explicitly distinguishes his poetic claim from the latter. If it sounds this way, it is because—as critics rather than poets—they can use only ordinary (that is to say, dualistic) language to account for a monistic use of language that is totally extraordinary. So their resortings to the religious analogies to convey metaphorically the substantive oneness in the word becomes inevitable. Below these religious analogies lies the central claim that the miracle of every true poem is the miracle of its meaning being not just *through* the work and not just *in* the work but at once *through* and uniquely *in* the work as body. And this is to maintain its functioning simultaneously as window and mirror. It is to push us beyond it and trap us within it, accomplishing the former only through accomplishing the latter: it performs the miracle in which a world enclosed by endlessly faceted mirrors, reflecting and re-reflecting images, is transformed—even as the mirrors fulfill their enclosing function —so that the mirrors somehow become windows opening again upon our everyday world, although through them that world never again can appear to us as it did before the mirrors originally shut us off from it.

All this is another way of stating the underlying principle of these theories, what I have elsewhere termed their "contextualism."[1] Negatively, this principle assumes the incapacity

---

[1] *The New Apologists for Poetry*, especially pp. 123–155, 182–201.

of normal discourse, for all its intentions of functioning transparently, to show more than typical abstractions from the reality it is to window. For this reality is an assemblage of endlessly unique individuals in endlessly unique relations in endlessly unique moments in time, while this discourse is limited in its referential power by the generic semantic character of its language and the generic systematic requirements of its logic. Positively, the principle asserts that each literary work must, as literature and not another thing, strive to become a self-sufficient system of symbols that comes to terms with itself—in effect, a unique philology, the "new word" of which Mallarmé spoke, whose definition is provided by the many old words as they together shut off their system. This shutting off compels the submissive and knowledgeable reader toward being utterly contained by the work, despite the fact that its references, taken atomistically, seem to be directed extramurally; despite, that is, the crucial—and obvious—relations between the words in the poem and the words as normally used in the cultural milieu that surrounds and nourishes the poem, between the "life" in the poem and the experiences of all who have to do with it as producer or consumer, between the forms and devices of the work and the received conventions and disciplines of an historically conditioned medium.

This extramural tendency of the parts of the poem taken by themselves indicates that each of us, in the history of our experience of the poem, begins by coming upon the consummate world of mirrors as simple, unmagical windows. As we enter the work, before its system gradually closes upon us, like shades of the prison-house upon Wordsworth's growing boy, it appears—like other discourse—to be composed of elements that mean to relate obviously and immediately to the world outside the walls. There are all sorts of relevancies to our literary awareness of a work, all sorts of information— biographical, psychological, ideological, technical, and in several ways historical—which we can ignore only at our peril. Most of all, perhaps, there is our own mature sensibility as human beings who have experienced. These are all indispensable to our apprehending simply what is going on in that thing which confronts us. As we begin to read we have no choice but to read referentially, relating what is inside the work to the world we know, treating the language of the work as we do other language, in effect as simple signs leading us transparently to their objects. How but in this bit-by-bit, hand-to-mouth way can we make our approach? Perhaps the writer began in much the same way, except that he had a special point of outside reference in his motive, his original intention that preceded the writing, the what-he-thought-he-meant-to-say-and-do in his work.

Still all we have in apprehending the extramural sign-relations is a knowledge and awareness of raw materials only. The test of poetry is whether or not it solicits us to end in another way of apprehending, whether or not it builds intramural relations among its elements strong enough to transform its language into new meanings that create a system that can stand up on its own. Thus for the contextualist the critic's task remains: to transfer us from sign to aesthetic symbol,[2] to show how the work—with what originally seemed to be its atomistic, independently referential elements—manages so to interrelate them, with their clouds of referential meaning trailing behind, as to create that self-sufficient, mutually supporting system that has the capacity to enclose the reader in total submission to it. But of course the critic must know

---

[2] A fuller argument that establishes the sense in which I am here using that confusing term "symbol" appears in Carl R. Hausman, "Art and Symbol," *Review of Metaphysics*, XV (1961), 256–270. His third definition of "symbol" (pp. 264–267) is that which I use here as aesthetic symbol as opposed to the merely "semiotic symbol," which is the first he defines (pp. 258–260) and is what I speak of here as "sign."

where the sign-functions leave off to know where the symbol-functions begin, and for this he needs all the knowledge of the world behind the signs that he can discover. This means knowledge of the world outside the poem, literary and real, the poet's and the critic's. That he must distinguish all that was outside from what *is* inside means he must allow the work its right to aspire to its own oneness and integrity (and have not almost all critics since Aristotle in their differing ways allowed as much?), although to do so he cannot rest in his knowledge of the signs out of which its oneness can grow but to which it cannot be reduced. If he can find a self-sufficient unity of internal relations out there, soliciting his apprehension—even if in his actual experience he may perhaps only momentarily transcend the referential relations he grabbed onto at the start as a way into the system—then he can hope to discover *all* that the symbols may mean here, in this unique, mutually modifying cluster of them. This "all," the "new word," can be revealed by no amount of sign-apprehension of all that they have meant elsewhere.

It is in just this spirit that Spitzer defines the role of the critic, whom he means to flatter with the name of "philologist." Arguing against the definition in Karl Shapiro's "A Farewell to Criticism" (1948), Spitzer asserts: "Instead of saying that poetry consists of 'not-words which, in their retreat from meaning, arrive at a prosodic sense-beyond-sense,' I would offer the suggestion that it consists of *words*, with their meaning *preserved*, which, through the magic of the poet who works within a 'prosodic' whole, arrive at a sense-beyond-sense; and that it is the task of the philologist to point out the manner in which the transfiguration just mentioned has been achieved. The irrationality of the poem need not lose anything at the hands of a discreet linguistic critic; on the contrary, he will work in accord with the poet (although with no regard to his approval), insofar as he will patiently and

I. RECENT LITERARY THEORY

analytically retrace the way from the rational to the irrational: a distance which the poet may have covered in one bold leap."[3] That Spitzer says in two sentences what I have been so long trying to maintain about the old words and the "new word" in poetry is evidence of the controlled compactness of his theoretical wisdom. What he says here of the ultimately irrational nature of the meaning of the poem, as this meaning arises out of the rational elements that enter the poem, will serve us with special cogency in our dealings with the farthest reaches of Shakespeare's *Sonnets*.

The contextualist must conclude, then, that the mark of a work's poetic value, like that of the sublime metaphor whose substantive transfer of properties, whose incarnation, amazes as it baffles us, is an integrity that allows it to persuade the submissive reader *toward* the utterly intramural experience even if his experience, in its inevitable waywardness and contingency, never quite gets there and if his criticism, with its dependence on normal discourse, can never fully account for it. We can admit that this utter containment may rarely if ever

[3] "Three Poems on Ecstasy," *Essays on English and American Literature*, pp. 141–142. Spitzer also relates this transformation of old words to the miraculism we have seen him defend earlier as he praises St. John of the Cross for "a poem in which mystery is presented with the greatest clarity and simplicity": ". . . unlike such a German mystic as Jacob Böhme, who resorts to new coinages in the attempt to express the inexpressible, adding the mystery of words to the mysterious experience, our poet, following the sober Latin tradition of all religious writing in Romance languages, is content with the stock of words already given by the language and, even here, limits himself to a restricted number. At the same time, however, he multiplies, by repetition, variation, and syntactical disposition, the density of the web of semantic interrelations, resuscitating the memories (memories of the soul and of the flesh) that are latent in popular terms. Thus, although the poem contains only familiar Spanish words which can be understood by the Spaniards of today as well as they were in the sixteenth century . . . these words have become endowed with a mystical depth which makes them appear as new words (though they *are*, *pace* Mr. Shapiro, the old words)." (p. 169)

actually occur, even to the most attentive of us, especially in long works. Still the critic can claim to discover the work's *capacity* to contain us, if only, less limited by our idiosyncrasies and our propensity to distraction, we were freer to comply with its demands. To the extent that it is a "new word," in its wholeness it has the capacity to house us, whether or not we actually have the perseverance as readers to shut the door. As reward if we do, it converts its windows to mirrors reflecting inward; but these are mirrors which finally, as enchanted windows, open outward again for us to an old world newly illumined. For this autonomous system, with its terminal and intramural relations, that make it complete, that work to keep us from going out into the world of ordinary meanings, ordinary logic, ordinary ideas, has its special and final value in illuminating our world of experience: the complexity of these internal relations allows it to be faithful to the actual stuff of our "pre-analytic" and thus pre-propositional or pre-ideological—yes, existential—experience as no other discourse can be. The contradictory forces, the dramatic tensions, whose simultaneous pressures trap us within the work, yet lead us outward to the world, since they are ultimately seen to reflect the existential tensions that no other discourse can afford to confront totally. Thus the poem (in the broad, Aristotelian sense) is seen as at once an insubstantial image and a substantive entity, at once leading somewhere else and leading terminally to itself, at once surrogate and sovereign, at once meaning and being: it is to be at once the word and the world. The polarities demanding reconciliation appear to require nothing less than a miracle.

The double thrust of this theory toward the *in* and the *through* may be more clearly understood if we look at each of its two antagonistic aspects in the purity of isolation. Writers have, as if for our convenience, pursued each of these aspects exclusively and to the end, in total opposition to the other. On the one side is the view of the poetic experience as cut off from the everyday world in response to a unique and nonreferential context. This view attributes transparent referentiality to nonpoetic discourse as window to the world, while it makes poetry into the enclosed set of mirrors, reflecting nothing but its internal relations. In its pure form—that espoused by the early I. A. Richards, for example, in his formulation of the emotive-referential dichotomy[4]—this view hands knowledge of the world over to nonpoetry, especially science, reserving poetry only for the manipulation of emotions. But the more mature contextualists—for example, any of the critics with whom I began—would never tolerate this view in its pure form, with its denial of poetry's relation to the world and its positivistic concession of all cognition to science. This view, in its single-mindedness and its firm pursuit of its own consequences, seems but a parody of their version of the mirror-aspect of poetry.

On the other side is the view that seems totally opposed to the first. In this view science is the enclosed system shut off from reality, and poetry alone is revelatory of our actual experience in the world. In its purest form—that put forward by Max Eastman, for example, in his attack on Richards[5]—this view emphasizes the contextual nature of systematic prose, especially science, and the freedom of poetry from the abstractions forced upon other discourse by the demands of logical system. Thus the referential-contextual dichotomy appears turned around: it is poetry that becomes the window on reality, giving us the "quality" of pure experience, and science

[4] See *Principles of Literary Criticism* (London, 1925), pp. 261–287; *Science and Poetry* (New York, 1926), pp. 66–79; and my discussion of these in *The New Apologists for Poetry*, pp. 57–63, 114–122, 182–184.

[5] See *The Literary Mind* (New York, 1931), especially pp. 297–317, and *The New Apologists for Poetry*, pp. 190–193.

the enclosed set of mirrors, a self-sufficient, hypothetical system of what experience must be constructed as being if it is to be manipulated successfully.[6] This pragmatic notion of science is interested not in what reality is but what can be done with it and to it; in its positivistic inversion of Richards' positivism, this notion has little use for the pure contemplation of experience that it allows to poetry, which in its unbridled formlessness is to capture the immediacy of sensory impressions. But though the sophisticated contextualists also want to allow poetry to reveal the fullness of existential reality, they are of course devoted to poetry's formal properties, which allow it to do more than reproduce the chaos of raw experience, properties that create a poem as a set of mirrors before it can function as window. As the early Richards seemed but a parody of their version of the mirror-aspect of poetry, so Eastman seems but a parody of their version of the window-aspect of poetry.

The value of seeing the contradictory, if oversimplified, positions of Richards and Eastman lies in what they show of the polarities that contextualism must contain in its appeal to miracle. The following diagram of the semantic functions of language in Richards and Eastman should sharpen our sense of their seeming incompatibility (see next page).

---

[6] This reminder that prose discourse does after all depend on context might seem to undercut all modern poetics based on a referential-contextual dichotomy. R. S. Crane claims as much in his "The Critical Monism of Cleanth Brooks," in *Critics and Criticism, Ancient and Modern*, ed. Crane (Chicago, 1952), pp. 100–105. Finally, however, the attribution of a context to nonpoetry does not disturb the *in-through* opposition. For however tight and controlling the context may be in nonpoetry, still we are dealing with a *through* meaning, one that is translatable, whose locus could be elsewhere and is not necessarily *in* these words in this order. For the context, being essentially logical and thus generic rather than unique and magical, does not produce the miracle that converts the words into body.

35

Richards (the mirror-aspect of poetry):

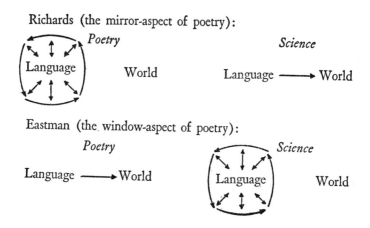

Eastman (the window-aspect of poetry):

But both, as I have said, are only parodies of the tendencies in contextualism which they represent so extremely, since in contextualism the other tendency is always there to qualify the one being pressed, so that in isolation each illustrates its own inadequacy more than anything else. Still the logical alternatives they present reveal the challenge to contextualism most nakedly; for in being mutually exclusive these alternatives remind us that walling in a discourse is hardly the most obvious way to open it outward. Yet this is the only way that contextualism, in accepting the difficulties resulting from its theoretical courage, will allow the poem to open outward. Contextualism will not look through any window that has not first proved itself a thoroughly self-contained world of mirrors. And it will not see the window except in the very act that sees all the inner reflections of the "mirrorized" world.

If a critic of contextualists sees this double movement as an attempt to have one's cake and to eat it too, he must be reminded that it is the way poetry seems to work in their experience with it that has forced the complexity of the theory upon them; that they must have the ordinary dimensions of language-as-sign—the semantic, syntactic, and logical dimensions—and then must lose these in the poem only to gain them back as most extraordinary dimensions functioning within a unique symbolic system that becomes its own sign only; that the analogies these dimensions of the poem bear to ordinary language-functioning is necessary to allow the reader initially to wander into the system, although once it closes, the analogous functions of normal language are seen as but weak parodies of the final, endlessly efficient functions of language as body in the poem; that once the word becomes body, becomes the world, the world itself is changed forever.

[ii]

All this the extreme and perhaps only consistent form of contextualism ought to assert, whether actual practitioners of it do or do not. Although the mystique in the double movement of contextualism will still arouse complaints, I am hopeful that the exposition of this doubleness will preclude the urging again of the many accusations against contextualism that result from misunderstanding, usually because its one movement toward the mirrorized world is seen as its total claim. On the other hand, however, it must be admitted that perhaps the accusations are invited, that our most influential practicing contextualists—the so-called New Critics—can all too often degenerate into formalism, stopping with the many-faceted mirror without getting through it at last to return to existence. This pattern of mutual misunderstanding has characterized the history of the New Critics in their relation to theoretical contextualism.

The serious and beneficial aspects of the New Criticism have long suffered from the distortions, indeed the parodies, of it created by its more heated followers as well as by its more heated opponents. Its enemies have complained that it is necessarily anti-scholarly and anti-historical in its denial of intentionalism; that, in the tradition of *l'art pour l'art*, it is intent on obliterating poetry's relation to life, society, morality, by shutting itself off by itself; that it is mental and verbal gymnastics performed out of sheer exhibitionism by Alexandrian creatures out of *The Dunciad*. Embattled academic liberals with extra-aesthetic motives have seen the movement as an agent of political and philosophic reaction: in its resort to miracle and its appeal to tradition and to absolute values they have seen a threat to progressive social-democracy and to secular, naturalistic humanism.

But, like most movements, this one has suffered more from friends than from enemies, as many of its followers too obligingly fulfilled these mistaken definitions. Often they did disdain history and scholarship with the consequent errors of recklessness. Often they did resort to an aestheticism that concerned itself exclusively with the display of interpretive virtuosity performed upon a literary art that was cut off from life, making of criticism an exercise, a sort of jig-saw puzzle where, as with jig-saw puzzles, the more pieces and the more minute pieces the greater the acclaim. Often too the position was used, not to satisfy the demands of the literary conscience, but to justify certain conservative political and religious commitments; and this despite the fact that, strangely enough, the doctrine itself, in its appeal to the containing tensions of irresolution, is beyond commitment and—as we have seen—even Manichaean in its implications, in its denial of rational affirmation. In addition, of course, there is, as always with the many followers of a fashionable movement, the pressing of an uncritical acceptance of principles into flat dogma, the consequence of the overripeness and institutionalization that are consequences of its successful sway. Still this state can freeze a dynamic theory into fashionable mechanics, can transform an ever-responsive organicism to a single formula indiscriminately imposed, with poets seen as fashionable favorites and unfashionable straw men that suggest it is poetic justice for the movement itself now to suffer from the vicissitudes of fashion. But, thanks to a time lag, even as the influence and serious reputation of the New Criticism wane, our universities and some of our journals, which have opened themselves to criticism only recently and self-consciously and indiscriminately, encourage the many uncreative practitioners of The Method, who seem dedicated to its Struldbrug-like longevity.

I trust my extended summary of the first principle of contextualism reveals how misleading both defenders and attackers of the New Criticism can be and have been in pressing their cases, reveals that below their claims and counter-claims is a serious and continuing claim which contextualism has upon our theoretical interest and respect. For it alone can with theoretical consistency escape one or another form of "imitationism"; that is, it alone has the theoretical advantage of finding in the literary work a unique locus of meaning—a meaning at once *in* and *through*—thus affording literature a unique function in culture. Of course, it must also claim the correlative disadvantage which constitutes more serious reason for worry than the objections that have concerned many of its attackers. For here is a theory that not only admits but must proclaim as its first principle its internal contradiction, the *in* and the *through*, the mirror *and* the window, a poetic context at once closed *and* uniquely open. It is what makes the appeal to miracle necessary, if perhaps theoretically unsatisfying, in that it is a substitute for explanation through an appeal to the unexplainable. One cannot blame theorists who have felt the need to seek alternatives that were rationally more satisfying.

Nevertheless, the rationalist's impatience with the mystique of contextualism need not lead to the attempt to wish away contextualism as a still significant shaping force, now that the existence of the New Criticism as an independent entity is about spent. But there are those who allow this impatience to lead them to treat contextualism as an unfortunate historical accident that did not ruffle essential theoretical issues and resettle them into substantial theoretical gains. They would prefer to return to the exclusive interest in poetry's window-function, forgetting the complications introduced by the interest of contextualism in poetry's internal reflections.[7] Fortunately, however, there are also more promising alternatives to contextualism which, while resisting it, do their work in a sophisticated awareness of its claims. But, as we shall see, these too end by appealing exclusively to poetry as an imitative art, as no more than a new dress for the "old word."

One could oversimplify the history of literary theory until our own time (but not altogether inaccurately) by characterizing it as the story of the many paths that have finally led to imitationism—or, to change the metaphor, of the many guises which imitationism has assumed. From the beginnings through much of the eighteenth century, one or another form of explicitly mimetic theory held sway, whether it advocated literal imitation or the imitation of universals or the imitation of other poets or the imitation of a morally ideal world or some combination of these. What these theories had in common was the central claim that the poem is essentially a translation of a meaning and form that already exist elsewhere, both prior to the poem and independently of it. But the expressionistic revolution engineered later in the eighteenth century by the champions of the organic imagination managed to produce only a deceptive alternative. The shift from the mimetic mirror, whose source of reality is outside, to the self-projecting lamp, whose source of reality is within, did not lead to a new way for poetry to have its meaning, as the major prophets and propagandists of this shift had led us to expect. Despite their statements claiming otherwise, they could not theoretically provide for a poem that was organic, even

---

[7] One of the more articulate and less extreme of these numerous spokesmen is Walter Sutton. See his two essays in *The Journal of Aesthetics and Art Criticism:* "The Contextualist Dilemma—or Fallacy?" XVII (1958), 219–229, and "Contextualist Theory and Criticism as a Social Act," XIX (1961), 317–325; and my own criticism of these essays in the same journal, "Contextualism Was Ambitious," XXI (1962), 81–88.

if the imagination was. Their philosophic idealism permitted the poet to be given a status and an independence beyond immediate reality, metaphysical reality, the history and traditions of his art, and externally imposed moral universals. He was made into a visionary, though his poem was no more than the vehicle that translated his rare, immediate, intuitive knowledge. But then the poem had still not become a unique, indispensable mode of discourse. Its meaning and form were still located outside and had their truth and justification in pre-poetic—or at least extra-poetic—terms.

Indeed, expression in this sense turned out to be a disguised form of imitation. True, the *object* of imitation was now an inward, mental one rather than an unyielding external one—and thus one that was more difficult to measure against its imitation in poetry. Still the poem dealt with a transcendent meaning that did not need the poem in order to achieve its definition. So long as its total meaning pre-existed its creation and its form, the poem had some imitative function, whether the historian labels the theorist proclaiming this function an expressionist or an imitationist. In sum, the expressionistic revolution may have enabled the poet to become immeasurably more creative than mimetic theory had allowed him to be; but it did nothing of the sort for his poem, which retained its handmaiden status even as its master was replaced. The poem would have to remain a new formal dress mechanically imposed on an old content.

It was left for the recent contextualists to claim as their major theoretical contribution the final union of the poem's meaning with the actual formal disposition of its elements. This union alone can permit the poem to become the sole locus of its unique meaning and thus to take on an organic, untranslatable character. It is this union and this character, earned theoretically only at great expense but promising considerable rewards for criticism, that are threatened with dissolution by alternatives to contextualism. Consequently, we must be on our guard against this tendency in these alternatives.

[iii]

One attractive way to obviate the contextualist's difficulties would be to invent an all-embracing eclecticism that could hold all sorts of antinomies by making all possibilities true in different ways from different views. Perhaps the most influential and exciting of such attempts is that presented by Northrop Frye. In the vast realms of his monumental and universal *The Anatomy of Criticism*, Frye, as the transcendent methodologist beyond intra-positional strife, rises above the parochialism of contextualism by placing it within one of the categories he so deftly manipulates. The organization of this majestic work and its justification in the "Polemical Introduction" reflect an unpartisan universality and inclusiveness, a concern with mutually exclusive perspectives and the limitations they impose upon subject-matter and definition, that suggest the procedures of modern analytic philosophy.

In the book there are brilliant analyses of possible positions, including among them something very like contextualism in the earlier portions of his Theory of Symbols, the second of his four theories. Arguing from an uncommitted catholicity of view, he examines the various partial perspectives, analyzing them in detail, seeing what each can include and what each must leave out, and banning any attempt to establish any one of them exclusively. As an analytic philosopher might, he denies that this procedure, the establishment of a single theory as the source for poetic value, can be of "scientific" merit, can be "empirical," can be anything more than tautological. Indeed, he must deny that it is dictated by anything more than mere subjective whim. So his is no theory so much as an argument for not having any. With Frye as with many of the analysts, the only question appears to be one of method, not of substance.[8] And of course both dismiss the possible validity of judgment, even though for the sublunary practicing critic aesthetic judgment would seem to be his crucial activity, if he takes as his primary function the guidance and improvement of taste. Frye makes the most of the similarities between the scientist's creation of a theory to account for his data (the order of nature) and the literary theorist's creation of a theory to account for his data (the order of literature). But he allows these similarities to override an all-important difference: unlike objects in the natural order, the objects in literature are expressly created as objects of value, and, to the extent that they are successfully literary, their value is their most important characteristic, their necessary cause. It ill befits the theorist, then, to begin by ignoring that value, to set himself so as not to account for it, and to treat only the mere occurrences of literary works as his phenomena. Here Frye's scientism is not enough.

So while the set of multiple awarenesses Frye gives us is most helpful in that it permits the humbling experience of seeing intellectual commitments and their limitations from perspectives outside our own, I fear that most of us cannot afford to commit ourselves exclusively to so Olympian a vista. As the analytic philosophers still leave substantive philosophy to be done, so Northrop Frye still leaves critical theory to be done by those of us who must, for the sake of letters, be partisans, who must move beyond prolegomena.

[8] Frye is too poetically keen to use that other weapon in the modern analysts' arsenal which, drawing upon their obsession with "ordinary language," relegates anything in extraordinary language to the emotive. Richard Foster seems somewhat influenced by this aspect of recent analytic philosophy. See his imputation of "mystical" (and philosophically irresponsible) motives to the New Criticism in such essays as "The Romanticism of the New Criticism" and "Criticism as Poetry," collected in *The New Romantics: a Reappraisal of the New Criticism* (Bloomington, 1962). I have criticized these charges in my review of this book: see *Criticism,* IV (1962), 369–372.

But Frye himself is also a partisan. The Northrop Frye that students of recent theory usually think of is a second one who, despite his catholic transcendence of positions, pronounces himself; who offers as an alternative to contextualism the openness of literary meaning to the archetypes of universal myth. This second is the Northrop Frye of much, though not all, of *The Anatomy of Criticism*, especially of the third essay on Archetypal Criticism or Theory of Myths, and the Mythical and Anagogic phases of the second essay on the Theory of Symbols, of which, as I have mentioned, the Literal-Descriptive and Formal Phases seem close to the New Criticism, though perhaps condescendingly so. And it is the Frye of many articles calling for a myth criticism.[9]

Frye conceives of all literature collectively as *an* order of language, a single autonomous mythic world-order (that is, word-order), independent of the analogous order of nature with which science deals. Like the mathematical world it resembles, the order of language has its own tables of equivalents, logics, causations. Yet, as Frye the analyst—the first Northrop Frye—must have it, the world-vision or the "total dream of man" which literature "imitates" has nothing in it of the factual or metaphysical—in short, of "knowledge" of the non-verbal order of nature—unless we fall into the "fallacy" of "existential projection" against which he warns, the error (and we shall see Cassirer and his followers fall into it) of thrusting the myth outward from the dream and allowing it to constitute our reality (*Anatomy*, pp. 63–65, 125–126). At once mystic and positivist, at once sympathetic and brilliant student of Blake and writer of the "Polemical Introduction," he proclaims both the glory and the limitations of the literary world-as-myth, sees it much like the Blakean or Yeatsian "system," but without their grandiose cognitive and

[9] One of the most lucid and helpful of these is among the more recent: "Myth, Fiction, and Displacement," *Daedalus* (Summer 1961), pp. 587–605.

metaphysical claims. This mythic order of language is the autonomous system of which the individual work partakes and, in effect, to which it refers. Criticism is to deal with nothing less than this total order. For the proper objects of Frye's criticism, in its aping of science, are not what he disdainfully terms "a huge aggregate or miscellaneous pile of discrete 'works.' " There are to be no unique "phenomena" since all phenomena must be dealt with only "as parts of a whole," "an order of words." As science does with the order of nature, with this order of words criticism must make "the assumption of total coherence," of a single, "totally intelligible body of knowledge," at whatever cost to the singleness—and, consequently, that most precious *dis*continuity—of the discrete work.[10]

Frye, then, can predicate autonomy not of the single work as entity but of the literary-mythic universe to which the single work refers and which it archetypically translates. His is a theory that finds meaning *through* the work only, not *in* and *through* it, since there can be nothing unique in the work; since, that is, it is "imitative," a translation whose essence is elsewhere. He need not worry about any sign-symbol or referential-contextual dichotomy since his entire literary universe, as mythic, is the autonomous unit, equally non-referential so long as we avoid the error of "existential projection." For all the brilliance and sophistication of this theory, does it not return literature to the same *way of meaning* as old imitation-theory had it, with only the referent changed—however important, of course, this change may be? The work itself cannot create through its symbolic system, through these words in this order; it can only refer to something extramural, since Frye constructs his walls not around the work but

[10] For these statements on the scientific obligations of criticism, see *The Anatomy of Criticism* (Princeton, 1957), pp. 15–17. For the comparison of literature to mathematics in my following paragraph, see *The Anatomy*, pp. 350–354.

I. RECENT LITERARY THEORY

around that collective, autonomous body of works or order of works, literature as a generic entity. The order of language being autonomous in the way that the order of mathematics is, the single work is as dependent on a coherent system that leads into and out of it as is the single mathematical equation on its system. There can be no discontinuity, no contextual containment, in either case. All of literature together comprises a gigantic collaborative enterprise, a not-altogether-voluntary joint-stock company. So if we ask where the unique, untranslatable, autonomous context is for Frye, we find that in denying it to the single work, he attributes it to this mystical Blakean entity, the mythic order of literature as a universal way of envisioning or imagining and transcribing into a language ever-varying and yet always the same.

This second Northrop Frye throws his shadow back upon the first and makes us qualify our view and judgment of him. For all the varying perspectives upon literature the first allowed, we see he allowed on the assumed analogy that criticism is to the order of language as science is to the order of nature. That is to say, the first Northrop Frye's exhaustive collection of "theories" ultimately springs, not from empirical analysis of the data, but from the Blakean mystique—however inconsistent it may be with the hardheaded positivistic approach he tries to persuade us of—that there exists one mythic linguistic order from whose "still center" all literature radiates and to which it returns in its imitation of "the total dream of man" (*Anatomy*, pp. 117–119). This central allegiance to Blake colors his grand view of the "theories" and makes it partial only, since it bypasses, or rather precludes, the critical judgment of each single context as unique. Thus his treatment of "Symbol as Monad" in the exciting and even apocalyptic "Anagogic Phase," in which language becomes its own universe, makes merely supercilious his suggestion of contextualism within the single literary work in the more modest

"Formal Phase," in which "Symbol" does not extend beyond the contained "Image."

It is precisely the all-embracing aspect of the system, its total ambition, that makes it finally specious, if strikingly impressive and even spectacular. Though it can be applied with special relevance to the work of a Blake or a Yeats, master poets who dedicate themselves to speaking the universal, perennial language, we may wonder about the critical propriety of treating other poets, differently dedicated, in this limited way. And then we may be led to wonder whether it does justice to the uniqueness of discrete poems of even Blake or Yeats. What if the more modest practitioners among us, non-Blakeans, who do not see Blake or Yeats as the archetype for all poets,[11] cannot adopt this mystical assumption about the transcendent, all-responsible, all-responsive unity of the sanctified body of literature—an assumption that seems to appeal to religious mystery more than the extremest claims of New Critics do, even though, it is true, our first and more positivistic Northrop Frye must deny any final cognition to this body? What if we rather think that literature must be like all other discourse until it makes itself otherwise, creates itself as otherwise through its own workings? that its obligation to its proper nature is to make itself otherwise, as our obligation as critics is to discover what it has made of itself, and how, and with what value for the rest of us? By "litera-

[11] Hazard Adams, who admits to being strongly influenced by Frye, makes my point for me most tellingly and perhaps too candidly. He openly puts the Blakean subscriber to the universal system at the very center of the properly "literary" rather than at the fringes. In "The Criteria of Criticism in Literature," *The Journal of Aesthetics and Art Criticism*, XXI (1962), 31–34, he lists the advantages of Frye's kind of position, concluding: "And perhaps most important, it would show that so-called 'occult' literature, making conscious use of 'mythical' and occult symbolism, should not be considered a curiosity for that reason but is *fundamentally* literary in its rigid delineation of the paradoxical forms and categories of all literature." (p. 33, his italics)

ture" here we would mean only a handy name, not itself an entity, to refer collectively to those "discrete works" that really concern us, that, however they illuminate one another, deepen the sign-meanings of one another, still must stand finally alone to be read and judged as autonomous symbolic systems. We would be restoring the referential-contextual opposition which Frye eliminates by removing all reference from the body of literature—and perhaps too, like the early I. A. Richards, from all language ("the order of words") except the rigorously scientific. We would be returned to the question about kinds of discourse, and to the consideration of what the unique and individual poem can in its oneness create, instead of trying to deal with that grandiose entity which we cannot specify, cannot locate in time or space or even in the unity of our experience of the poem—that total world-dream or world-as-dream that deprives the poem of its singleness and criticism of its need to evaluate. It is not surprising that Frye can blandly dismiss judgment—indeed he must—since his interest is always centered (still-centered) in literature as one order and not on the dynamic, discontinuous unpredictability of the unique poem in its workings. Here is a strange return to universals for this modern skeptic—and a loss of the concrete for which the New Criticism did so much and the celebration of which I had thought would be its most indispensable legacy.

In a spirit much like Frye's, Edwin Honig more explicitly seeks a reasonable alternative to contextualism and its anti-scientific miraculism. In his *Dark Conceit: the Making of Allegory* (1959), Honig works to deny the contextualist's distinction between symbol and allegory, and for reasons that Frye should have helped make clear for us. For if one assumes—with Honig, as with Frye—that there is no referential-contextual opposition since all literature partakes of *the* mythic order, refers to it, imitates it, then there can be no distinction between sign (or allegory) and symbol, as I

48

made it earlier, and all literature finally translates into allegory. There can be only differences in degree concerning how thoroughly and explicitly or how cryptically works relate to this order, from the most conventional and public allegory to the most private. The latter the romantic may wish to dignify with the name of symbolism in his disdain for the open intellectuality of obvious allegory. Thus Honig apparently limits the notion of symbol to what it means for the French Symbolists instead of allowing it to mean what it has meant for organic and contextualist theory. And for him the New Critic is the defensive creature he terms the "symbolist-in-retreat," who, in fear of science and reference, has deluded himself into a justification of art in terms of a distinction that does not exist. In dealing with specific works, Honig achieves impressive results on these assumptions, assumptions which, however, I suspect will stand or fall with Frye's. Like Frye, he must find the locus of meaning outside the work which, thus deprived of its uniquely creative powers, must be contented with an imitative role.

[iv]

Philip Wheelwright, on the other hand, tries to open literature's mythic dimensions without violating the integrity of the poetic context. We have already seen Wheelwright as an ally of the New Criticism. While he tries to move beyond it, he means to do so in accordance with its special orientation to poetry and its language. In his major work, *The Burning Fountain* (1954), he treats literature as a form of "expressive discourse" coordinate with myth, ritual, and religion; he even—unlike Frye, and I think too easily and not quite judiciously—allows them all to yield "expressive truth." They become alternatives to "literal discourse" and "literal truth," which in his anti-positivism he leaves to the enemy, science.

Wheelwright proceeds through anthropological studies of

myth and ritual, and their relations to religion and literature, trying to get at meaning by way of contextualism with his twin concepts of "depth meaning" and "radical metaphor."[12] He wants to use both the *in* and the *through* for his "expressive" language in finding the locus of its meaning. But here he fails: his terms are too large, his analogies among the several varieties of expressive language too broad, so that he falls victim to the self-deceiving dangers of expressionism that I have traced. How can myth, ritual, religion, and literature mean in the same way unless this meaning is not tied to language itself and its limitless possibilities for manipulation and significant play? He does say that expressive meaning must be *"in and through . . ."*—but *"in and through* the emotions" (*The Burning Fountain*, p. 48), for he cannot quite say "in and through language" so long as this way of meaning is to apply to more than literature. His several varieties of expressive language must *mean* in the same way although most of them are not really dependent upon language at all—that is, controlled and figured language, tropistic language, language that has its meaning in and through *it*.

Wheelwright here suffers from the difficulty which inevitably afflicts idealist poetics and is especially troublesome in this neo-Kantian version of it. In essential agreement with D. G. James, Wheelwright wants "to accept this Coleridgean doctrine of the continuity between man's primary (or constitutive) imagination and his secondary (or poetic) imagination. . . ."[13] But if we attribute the essential symbolizing power, the visionary power, of creativity, to man's generally

[12] For an extended critique of these concepts, which has influenced my own treatment of Wheelwright, see Eliseo Vivas, "A Semantic for Humanists," *Sewanee Review*, LXIII (1955), 307–317.

[13] *The Burning Fountain* (Bloomington, 1954), p. 77. See Note 1, pp. 371–372, for his approval of D. G. James on Coleridge (in *Scepticism and Poetry*, London, 1937). I have criticized this view at length in *The New Apologists for Poetry*, pp. 98–110.

constitutive act of normal perception, then how can we allow the poetic context—these words in this order—to be symbolic or creative in a unique way? In other words, if the distinction between symbol and nonsymbol (or mere sign) is made before the act of making poetry, and if the symbol is attributed to all human constitutive perception—and to its constitutive agency, language—then no way is left to distinguish between symbol and nonsymbol (or mere sign) within the act of language, within the various modes of discourse. Indeed there are, in effect, no varieties at all within discourse once all language, by its mere virtue as language, is made symbolic. Where, then, can there be the special *in*-and-*through* symbolism of art, except as an intensification by degree of the general ("through") use of language? And here, where all language is given symbolic properties, with the consequent denial of a difference in kind between aesthetic and non-aesthetic symbols (that is, symbols created by the secondary or by the primary imagination, respectively), here Wheelwright is closest to Frye and Honig. Here too, interestingly, he urges his one serious complaint against New Critical doctrine: that it emphasizes too exclusively the synthesizing power of the poetic imagination and poetic language at the expense of the imagination's broader powers.

Wheelwright produces some exciting and revealing studies, and pretty much contextualist studies, but I must ask, as I did of Frye, where the context must finally be for him—the unique, untranslatable, autonomous context. It cannot be *in* "the right words in the right order" as well as *through* them, as the in-and-through contextualist would have it. Let us try the expressive statement Wheelwright uses as example: "God exists" (pp. 292ff.). Surely he would admit this as a *through* meaning only, not as an *in* meaning, since it is capable of translation and of a meaning apart from the words. His answer would likely be that, in accordance with a coherence theory rather than a correspondence theory, the statement has meaning only within the context of the religious experience or vision that thrusts it forth. Good enough. But we see where his context must be: not in the symbolic structure of the work but in man's vision or experience that precedes and transcends the work. Despite his dismissal of the correspondence theory, he gives us an imitation theory still, in that the *through* meaning has its essence elsewhere.

This poetics becomes an apologia for mysticism, for a vision or an experience that claims truth on intuitive grounds. Though a philosopher of language, Wheelwright has returned to Shelley's divine source, "the burning fountain" of *Adonais* that is his title, as he has returned to Shelley's extravagant *Defence of Poetry*. Expressive truth ends by depending upon its source rather than upon its linguistic form; it can even turn out to be a propositional claim to truth that Wheelwright does not feel should be subjected to the rational critique to which we would normally demand it submit. It sets up shop across the street from the literal truth of science and arbitrarily claims certain exemptions.[14] This is not the place to argue these claims; but, just or unjust, they are vastly different from the primary claim of this theorist who, in the spirit of contextualism, embraces, for cognitive reasons, "the thesis . . . of *the ontological status of radical metaphor*" (p. 97). It may be that myth criticism, by the nature of its

[14] I have argued elsewhere (*The New Apologists for Poetry*, pp. 174–175) in greater detail that the romantic opposition between intuitive or imaginative truth and propositional truth is a false one, since the first is based on the source of the perception and the second on the form it takes in language. As with "God exists," intuitions can take a propositional form. What characterizes truth as intuitive is not its formulation but the way in which it was apprehended. Thus the proper antagonist to intuitive or imaginative truth is not propositional truth but rational truth. And against propositional truth should be posed that which is not propositional in its linguistic form—the contextualist version of poetry, as New Critics ought to argue.

objectives that must open the context of the literary work outward to a wider context, cannot with consistency come
through the contextualism of the New Criticism, since as
myth criticism it must merge the language of poetry into a
larger vision that not only precedes the poem but pre-empts
it.

[v]

The neo-Kantian view of culture and reality, as these are
humanly constituted through symbols, also furnishes the
ground for another approach. We can describe it with that
tired phrase "the new historicism," meaning by it neither
the nonhistoricism of pure New Criticism nor the old historicism of pre-New Criticism. It is an attempt, in accordance
with certain notions derived from the neo-Kantian Ernst
Cassirer and from Existentialism, to return literature to history and existence by treating it as a specially empowered
bearer of historical, social, and moral vision. Of course, all
historicism has seen literature as a mode of revealing culture.
But older historicisms have usually seen literature as a dramatic translation of notions already formulated in culture. Thus
Lovejoy related literature to the history of ideas in a way which
had the ideas, whether inside or outside literature, whether
entering or emerging from literature, as essentially identical.
But the "new historicist," like Cassirer, rather sees a culture
as a complex of unformulated forces which is inaccessible
except through that culture's symbolic structures, of which
literature is a primary and most useful representative.

Nevertheless, to the extent that it sees literature as no more
than the bearer of an awareness that has its locus elsewhere,
the "new historicism" retains historicism's inherent reluctance
to allow the poem to do its creative, its more than imitative,
work. The approach often seems influenced more by European
Stylistics than by New Criticism. Its best model is probably

Auerbach's *Mimesis*, which we have already looked at in another connection. This work investigates which symbols constituted the reality of various historical moments; but it can find these symbols anywhere: in literature, sub-literature, philosophy, gardens, hair-dos, in a phrase or a brushstroke as in an entire work. Erwin Panofsky uses his "iconology" in a parallel way in the plastic arts. I find a similar intention in recent work by Frederick J. Hoffman and Roy Harvey Pearce. Hoffman has now produced several startling essays on violence, death, and selfhood in recent literature.[15] In the best of these there is continually the penetrating discovery of the very pulse of a culture's sensibility in the nerves and sinews of the work. Pearce, like Hoffman, sees the primacy of an inward historical vision that translates itself, or gets reflected, into poetry as into other forms of discourse, a vision that projects its symbols outward into all forms of cultural expression; but neither of them seems to grant to the manipulation of language within the peculiarly poetic context that special power, perhaps shared only with the media of the other arts, to generate awarenesses of existential tension. Indeed, in his joint essay with Sigurd Burckhardt, Pearce expressly denies this power, and just after Burckhardt seems to me to have demonstrated it most remarkably: "Note well that I avoid deliberately the phrase 'poetic use of language'; for it seems to me that poems are simply examples of a special, concentrated use of what some modern linguistic scholars call 'non-casual

---

[15] These are portions of a new book, *The Mortal No: Death and the Modern Imagination* (Princeton, 1964). Among the most exciting are "The Moment of Violence: Ernst Jünger and the Literary Problem of Fact," *Essays in Criticism*, X (1960), 405–421; "The Assailant and the Victim: Some Definitions of Modern Violence," *Centennial Review*, V (1961), 223–238; "The Self in Time," *Chicago Review*, XV (1961), 59–75. See also his "Form and Circumstance: A Study of the Study of Modern Literature," in *Approaches to the Study of Modern Literature; Proceedings of the Conference in the Study of 20th-Century Literature*, Michigan State University, 1961, pp. 3–16.

utterances' and are therefore still quite within the purview of language as we use it day-to-day."[16] If, in light of this denial, we ask again, this time of Pearce, where he finds the unique, autonomous, untranslatable context, he must give us essentially the answer that Auerbach gave in *Mimesis* in a description of the cultural matrix of an historical moment that, strikingly, sounds very much like a description by Cleanth Brooks of the closed context of a poem:

"When people realize that epochs and societies are not to be judged in terms of a pattern concept . . . when, in other words, they come to develop a sense of historical dynamics, of the incomparability of historical phenomena and of their constant inner mobility; when they come to appreciate the vital unity of individual epochs, so that each epoch appears as a whole whose character is reflected in each of its manifestations; when, finally, they accept the conviction that the meaning of events cannot be grasped in abstract and general forms of cognition and that the material needed to understand it must not be sought exclusively in the upper strata of society and in major political events but also in art, economy, material and intellectual culture, in the depths of the workaday world and its men and women, because it is only there that one can grasp what is unique, what is animated by inner forces, and what, in both a more concrete and a more profound sense, is universally valid: then it is to be expected that those insights will also be transferred to the present and that, in consequence, the present too will be seen as incomparable

---

[16] "Poetry, Language, and the Condition of Modern Man," *Centennial Review*, IV (1960), 15n. See all of Pearce's portion of this essay (pp. 15–31) and his "Historicism Once More," *Kenyon Review*, XX (1958), 554–591. His admirable and ambitious study, *The Continuity of American Poetry* (Princeton, 1961) exemplifies this approach, with an emphasis—indicated in his title—on cultural continuity among a community of works, which is directly opposed to my own emphasis on the unique discontinuity of the individual work. See especially pp. 6–12, from his Foreword.

and unique, as animated by inner forces and in a constant state of development. . . ."[17]

Here is an admirable and exciting statement, but not one that, for all its cultural organicism, can find a uniquely expressive context in the dynamic linguistic interrelations of the literary work. The uniqueness and untranslatability that a Brooks would attribute to the context of the poem, Auerbach has attributed to the historical moment, and in many of the same words. Terminology in this quotation like "dynamics," "incomparability," "constant inner mobility," "vital unity," "whole . . . reflected in each," "cannot be grasped in abstract and general forms," "animated by inner forces," "a more concrete and a more profound sense," "unique and incomparable"—these should have a familiar ring to those familiar with New Critical paeans to the poetic context. Yet Auerbach attributes them not uniquely to poetry or the arts but to the historical moment that manifests itself in all of a culture's activities, of which poetry is but one representative form coordinate with the rest (not only "in the upper strata of society and in major political events but also in art, economy, material and intellectual culture, in the depths of the workaday world and its men and women").

Panofsky gives us a more transparent statement restricting the expressive powers of art to those of non-art, as he relates his notion of "iconology" to the symbolism of Cassirer: "In thus conceiving of pure forms, motifs, images, stories and allegories as manifestations of underlying principles, we interpret all these elements as what Ernst Cassirer has called 'symbolical' values. . . . we deal with the work of art as a symptom of something else which expresses itself in a countless variety of other symptoms, and we interpret its compositional and iconographical features as more particularized

---

[17] *Mimesis*, trans. Willard R. Trask (Princeton, 1953), pp. 443–444. I am indebted to my student, Keith Kessel, for making me aware of this passage.

evidence of this 'something else.' The discovery and interpretation of these 'symbolical' values (which are often unknown to the artist himself and may even emphatically differ
from what he consciously intended to express) is the object
of what we may call 'iconology' as opposed to 'iconography.' "[18]
The word "symptom" here is thoroughly symptomatic of
where the context is. We must worry, despite any sophisticated
disclaimers, about how "new" this sort of historicism finally
can be, about how it, any more than its ancestors, can avoid
the charges of imitationism which have always led some
theorists to the sense of its inadequacy.

We have another version of the difficulty which I originally
found in Wheelwright, and it stems here as it did there from
the neo-Kantian epistemology. It is the difficulty of deciding
between literary symbolism and the symbolism which is all
language. For most of us, Ernst Cassirer is largely responsible
for the notion that the mind in its symbolizing powers becomes a constitutive agent, that man constitutes his reality,
and a culture its reality, through the symbolic structures that
he creates and it creates. But the idealist's problem remains:
if man constitutes his reality through symbols, then how is
literature specially or differently constitutive? If all language
is creative, then how is the poem's context uniquely so? As
with Wheelwright, we are with the new historicists troubled
by the need to keep symbolism from being too broad for
literature and thus not dependent on the literary context, not
dependent on the need to be *in* it as well as *through* it.

None of this is intended to withhold my agreement from
Kant's central claim about the constitutive powers of the mind
in its perception or from Cassirer's central claim about the
constitutive powers of language in its symbolization. But these
claims are clearly epistemological, while my interest is phenomenological only. That is to say, I am concerned neither

[18] *Meaning in the Visual Arts* (New York, 1955), p. 31.

with the genesis of our vision of the world, however we may originally project our categories upon the sense-data that confront us, nor with the originally constitutive powers of language as it is created by human culture. I am rather concerned with whether or not, on the existential level, our normal adult vision, with all its habitual automatism, may properly be described as creative; and whether or not language as we normally use it, drawing upon the scrap-heap of the pre-formed molds our culture has accumulated, has any life, any constitutive power. I would maintain that, for the adult, the things he senses are (for all practical purposes and apart from epistemological considerations about what is *really* and aboriginally happening) found as being *there* and are hardly "created"; and that, similarly, for the adult in an advanced culture which has a repository of words, phrases, and syntactical forms bequeathed by an originally creative language, the symbols he uses are for him dead signs which he automatically picks up to satisfy his inexact needs. If, in his late culture, he does restore constitutive power to his language and his vision—really two aspects of the same act—he is creating the freshness of context that is poetry. But the power can be found only *in* and *through* his new symbolization, and as such it will add to culture's repository where others can pick it up to increase their own awarenesses. It is for this reason that, despite the claims of neo-Kantian epistemology for the universally constitutive powers of the mind and its language, I can claim a unique phenomenological creativity for the special language of art.

[vi]

Thus it is that one may see the need for another variety of "new historicism" that would be dependent upon contextualism and would want to extend it without violating its essential spirit. If the new historicists we examined earlier finally see literature merely as the bearer of its culture's historical vision, this variety would see literature as that which originally formulates this vision through its context and makes it available to its culture. Finally there is of course no denying some imitative role to literature: since history pre-exists literature, literature must in some sense imitate it. There can, then, be no question about history getting into literature: it is the very stuff of literature which, after all, cannot be created *ex nihilo*. But this history that enters literature as its raw material is the living, felt, pulsing history of breathing men and not the static formulae of ideology. So it is history as existential force that gets into literature by being there first; it is history as institutionalized in ideology that comes after, thanks in part to what literature shows us.

Eliseo Vivas is central to this line of thought, as we see in many of his essays, especially in "The Object of the Poem."[19] His key terms are "*sub*sistence," "*in*sistence," and "*ex*istence." The prefixes indicate the three stages he sees in the developing relation of historical meaning to language and poetry: meaning that is *under* or before language, meaning that is *in* the language of the poem, meaning that comes *out* of the poem into our language generally. Accordingly, I would translate these, if I may tear them from the context of Vivas' metaphysic, as (1) meanings and values potentially within a culture though not yet analyzed, realized in institutions, or perhaps even understood; (2) these meanings and values as they are grasped *in* and *through* the total intramural structure of the poem, as the mirror-window, though they can never appear thus elsewhere; and (3) these meanings and values as they are extracted from the work to enter culture by being translated and thinned for use.

For purposes of explication, I dare to oversimplify a single

[19] In *Creation and Discovery* (New York, 1955). Among his other relevant essays, see especially "Literature and Knowledge" and "What is a Poem?" from that volume and "The Constitutive Symbol," *D. H. Lawrence: the Failure and Triumph of Art* (Evanston, 1960).

case. For "subsistence" let us think of the indefinable subterranean forces at work in the Renaissance. Some of these find their way into every facet of the complex structure that is Marlowe's *Faustus*. Here, and only here, this special grouping of them achieves absolute "insistence." If one wants the full array of these forces in their interrelations, he must come here for them. But the cultural interest in ideology can abstract from the complex of forces in the play and come up with the notion of "Faustian man" which it can use anywhere, in an endless variety of contexts. The forces can thus achieve Vivas' "existence," though we must still return to the play for the whole of what it is to be Faust.

Let me expand a bit. In the Renaissance all sorts of pressures and counter-pressures, feelings and counter-feelings, impulses and counter-impulses, become operative in Western culture, some of them not yet recognized or identified, and surely not ordered. Yet they are operatively there, below the level of culture's ideologies and institutions, though potentially they are a source for changes in both. Can they then be said to exist as yet? It depends on how we mean "exist." They do exist in that, in some subterranean way, they are a functioning force in culture, part of the unanalyzed, received world-as-stimulus; but they do not exist in that there is as yet no "they," since there is as yet no definition, no bracketing, of them to make them an entity, to institutionalize them into official being. In Vivas' language, they "subsist." Now a cluster of these existentially functioning, nonentity "somethings" becomes aesthetically grasped and organized in a unique whole, a self-sufficient poetic context, Marlowe's *Faustus*. The earlier *Faustbook* bears certain sign-relations to it, but in its total symbolic structure of language and action this *Faustus* becomes at once the container and the synthesizing creator of these resistant, tensional forces. It is both mirror of them and window to them. To use Vivas' term, they "insist" in the poem and have their locus only there. At the crucial moment when the poem becomes one, its historical meanings must become meta-historical if they are themselves to become normative of the intellectual categories that characterize the cultural history that follows. Now that the poet has grasped these data in their fullness and has displayed them to his culture, or in a sense created them for it, they can play a more institutional role in that culture. The culture can extrapolate from the "insistent" totality a thinned version of that totality and put it to use. For the culture must sacrifice the meaning *in* for the meaning *through*. The more universally applicable notion of "Faustian man" is born and the modern world has a new series of ideas to help it intellectually to understand itself. The nonentity "somethings" now can be referred to *through* language: they have been recognized, identified, labeled; and in a discursive—if somewhat diluted—form they can play their part in the march of culture's institutions. They have attained full "existence,"[20] in Vivas' terms, except that, alas, so much of their vital substance has been lost that culture has only the shadow of their operative vitality to deal with in its discursive terms. The "existence" which becomes the entity is but a parody of their total nonentity existence (or rather "subsistence") which precedes and still underflows what institutional culture must translate them into, if it is to make use of them in its limited way. Still we must return to Marlowe's *Faustus* itself, to all the interrelations within its structure and its technical virtuosity, as their unique vehicle and untranslatable definition. Art is still where it was with Kant, between the percept and the concept, here between the unrecognizable operative forces

[20] Vivas' use of "existence" is troublesome for me and, in conjunction with my own use of "existential," may cause the reader some confusion, because my "existential," being pre-propositional, is really close to his "subsistence," while his "existence" has become that for him because it is now propositional. Thus for his metaphysical terms, "subsistence," "insistence," and "existence," my terms would be the existential, the aesthetic-thematic, and the propositional, respectively.

and the too recognizable abstraction from them. At a later moment in culture, with new "subsistent" historical forces operating, the Faust of the *Faustbook* and of Marlowe and many of the "existent" meanings stemming from them enter the work of Goethe as signs, and there emerges a new *Faust*, a new unique structure of "insistent" meanings which a later culture, in search of discursive understanding, will prey upon but to which, fortunately, it can always return when in its less efficient moods it can afford nothing less than authenticity. All these meanings of the several moments together, "insistent" and "existent," enter the work of Thomas Mann at a still later moment, with similar results both for art (a new "insistent" meaning) and for the discursive institutions of culture (a new "existent" meaning).[21]

Of course, none of this is to deny the limitations of the critic as he works with his own discursive language. He cannot reproduce the work's "insistent" meanings since his language contains only "existent" ones. But still his use of signs can crudely point our way toward the new and revealing con-

---

[21] The indebtedness of this position to Benedetto Croce should be obvious. The relation of "insistence" to "existence" is in crucial ways an echo of Croce's relation of the intuitive to the conceptual (see, for example, *Aesthetic*, trans. Douglas Ainslie, New York, 1922, pp. 1–31), although I would hope his distinction has been extended and detailed considerably. However, the claims being made here still seem unique to me in their total identification of "insistent" meaning with the actual disposition of the materials of the work. Vivas can make this identification total as Croce cannot. Despite Croce's identification of intuition with expression, his philosophical idealism prevents him from allowing truly transforming powers to the poetic medium. So he must reduce to secondary and only auxiliary importance what he thinks of as merely technical devices and must retain the pure intuition (and expression!) as an entirely "spiritual" affair, lest it be reduced to a mere "physical fact." He is led to a distinction, hard for nonidealists to comprehend, between "expression" and "externalization," with the latter seen as no more than a physical translation of spiritual vision (see *Aesthetic*, pp. 95–97, 111–117). That Vivas' "insistent meaning" has its unique locus in the poetic context is what distinguishes this position and makes it a position we could not expect to come upon prior to the New Criticism.

figurations. He—and we with him—must realize how far from exhaustive his work is with its "existent" formulae. For example, it must not be thought that the literature of what I have elsewhere called the "tragic vision" can no longer be created "insistentially" to the extent that I have successfully formulated it and laid out its categories in "existent" language. Nothing could be greater nonsense, except in the case of the uncreative author who searches for formulae to substitute for the "insistential" obligations he incurs as poet. The really new "insistent" creation will reveal at once the inadequacy of the seeming exhaustion of possibilities by any "existent" framework and the false pretensions of any framework that would claim more.

Vivas' own work—for example, his recent study of Lawrence—has reflected this theoretical approach. Perhaps the most startling examples of the approach that I know occur in the writings of Sigurd Burckhardt, among them the first half of the two-part joint article he shared with Roy Harvey Pearce, "Poetry, Language, and the Condition of Modern Man," to which I have referred earlier.[22] Here, despite Pearce's claim to the contrary in his portion, Burckhardt reveals the special power of poetry as a unique mode of discourse. This is an exciting *tour de force* that proceeds through analyses of poems on a similar subject by Robert Herrick, Gerard Manley Hopkins, and Wallace Stevens, out of which he spins a history of Western sensibility—but out of the very texture, the technical devices, every conceivable formal element, and yet the formal element never quite formal, because the form creates vision, creates existential stance.

[22] *Centennial Review*, IV (1960), 1–15. In many ways as brilliant, and with many of the same virtues, is his essay, "The Poet as Fool and Priest," *ELH*, XXIII (1956), 279–298, which I have discussed in my opening section. There are several others as fine, mainly on Shakespeare. Much of what I say about Burckhardt in what follows would apply, if with less force, to my essay on Pope, "The 'Frail China Jar' and the Rude Hand of Chaos," *Centennial Review*, V (1961), 176–194.

As I have observed earlier, for Burckhardt here and elsewhere, each poet becomes creator of his own unique philology in his poem, a philology in which every reflective meaning has substantive cause, in which every phonetic accident is transformed into substantive causation, for this is an endlessly teleological world in which there is no accident. Configurations of sound and meaning create the illusion of language going it on its own, becoming a total object itself, having its own world of multiplying relations, taking on what Burckhardt calls "corporeality." For this variety of new historicism alone, if such it be, while the miraculously simultaneous functions of the *in* and the *through* are still unresolved, their significance has been extended, not surrendered.

I have deliberately separated Burckhardt from Pearce despite their sharing the one article I have mentioned and their implicit claim in it to share one position, because I think the two of them demonstrate the difference between the two "new historicisms" I have suggested. There can be a great difference between moving from history to literature and moving from literature to history, that is, between finding the locus of the inviolable context out of which the critic must operate in the cultural complex and finding it in the language complex of the literary work. This essentially is the difference between the two "new historicisms" I have tried to describe and distinguish. In moving from the historical context to literature, one may come to the work with too good an idea of what he is looking for, of what forces it must reflect or— to be theoretically candid—what forces it must "imitate"; thus there must be an inhibiting of the empirical act that can allow literature to do its own work. But in moving from the literary context to history, the critic can learn from the work what it was in the culture that he as historian should be looking for, even if without the work's illuminations he could not see it. From the front end of history, our vantage point, the poet's activity may indeed look like the imitation of what has already been formulated elsewhere in culture; but to the extent that he has imitated truly existential and pre-conceptual forces, one cannot know what was being imitated until after the poet has made it perceptible—which is to say, after he has created it to show what it was he imitated.

In one of his most definitive essays,[23] Spitzer revealed his simultaneous concern about both functions and both contexts I have been speaking of, the cultural and the poetic, and his desire to engage in both of them in dealing with poetry. But he revealed also, although less consciously, the extent to which the two contexts reflect different and apparently unreconcilable critical assumptions. With more theoretical naïveté than we might have expected but with a critic's candor that betrays only the best of motives, he tries to have at once the historicist's and the critic's view. First, Spitzer sees the poem—aside from its contextual nature as aesthetic entity—as having vision ("of a world radically different from our everyday and workaday world of ratiocination and practicality"); and this vision allows the work to be termed "poetic." Secondly, this vision can be made representative, a distillation of the vision of an historical period ("it offers an overly rich condensation of the whole wealth of medieval thought and feeling about one of the basic forces of mankind"); and this characteristic he terms, in quotation marks, "great." Thirdly, the work can be marked "by its self-sufficiency and organic perfection which allow it to stand out as an independent whole"; and this characteristic enables it to be termed "artistic." But how to relate its historic or representative greatness to its artistry as methods of making its poetic vision more available? Can it be "great" without being "artistic"? (We may assume its "poetic" capacity for

[23] *"Explication de Texte* Applied to Three Great Middle English Poems," *Essays on English and American Literature,* pp. 193–247. For the following discussion see especially pp. 216, 218–219, 233.

vision exists prior to aesthetic and historical questions, although if it is a proper poem this vision is defined by and is available only in and through the total context.) Spitzer has crossed, with insufficient awareness of conflict between the consequences of each, from the existential to the poetic context. But the history of literary theory demonstrates that it is indeed difficult to do better—as, with others' help, I am trying to do here.

Except in the arts, the existential forces, admittedly active everywhere, cannot achieve that precise and constitutive symbolization which gives them an identity in culture. Or so the second new historicism, in contrast to the first and beyond even Spitzer, must maintain. Nevertheless, I would hope that, in actually working with literature, this difference between the two new historicisms may finally prove not to be so essential, or at least so apparent. For it seems to me that the two approaches, in their common dedication to poetry's role in an existential anthropology—which is what the new historicisms really turn out to be—can be made into strong allies.

[vii]

So I emphasize again contextualism's affirmation of the miraculous powers of poetry as both mirror *and* window, as I emphasize the special value of that affirmation. In resorting to the metaphor (or should I not, with more precision, say the analogy?) of the mirror and the window to describe how the word, though always mere word, is yet rescued from its empty status as sign by being endowed with substance, I am echoing Shakespeare's use of this metaphor as it becomes the force allowing the miraculous transformation in the *Sonnets* from appearance to reality. Or so we shall find when we come to treat his word—which, for Shakespeare, is to say his world —rightly; that is, when we treat the *Sonnets* as a metaphorical entity, a single body of mythology, of systemic meaning.

66

For the miracle is in Shakespeare's method as well as in the subject of his metaphor: the metaphor, in the manner of its meaning, functions as mirror and window even as its substance asserts the union of mirror and window as entities. The metaphor in effect justifies itself by demonstrating its meaning through the way in which it functions. Thus I must use the *Sonnets* here, not as mere demonstration of a poetics (though they serve in this way), but, more profoundly, as an allegory of the method, a metaphorical foreshadowing of its farthest reaches, its most ambitious claims.

Before turning to the mirror-window relations in the *Sonnets,* let me renew finally our awareness of the mirror-window relations in a poem, as contextualism views it, and of their consequences upon the cognitive claims of the poem. Let me do so by way of a not very subtle allegory that may clarify these relations.

A man, dazed from the confusions and dissatisfactions arising from his need to act in the world and among its objects, wanders in weariness out of the busyness of that world and its pressures. While wandering, he comes upon a glass house which he can see is filled with objects of its own. Perhaps it is a contemporary museum, constructed, it would appear, to represent the activities of his world. He is drawn to the house, attracted by the objects inside. He stops outside and looks in through the window-walls: he sees the objects, illuminated by the light of day, as mere replicas of the outside world—*his* world—common but attractive. For while mere replicas, in their reduced form and unreal materials they demand only his contemplation of them rather than his action upon them. They draw him in. Once inside, he becomes fascinated by the objects, even though the source of this fascination lies in their resemblance to their archetypes in the world, in the crafty subtlety with which these miniatures reflect this relation. So he continually glances from the objects to the window-walls and through them to the outside, the source of all light and all reality. He compares what he has found inside to what is outside, whether in his immediate view or in his memory.

Gradually, in his returns to the objects, he comes to feel that there may be light emanating from within the objects themselves. Still he persists in stopping his contemplation of them and putting a halt to the growing mystification by looking up and out through the window-walls. But then the time comes when his absorption in the objects becomes so intense as to lead him to neglect to make that reassuring upward and outward glance. And presto! He finally does look up again but no longer out; for he finds the window-walls have closed inward, have been transformed to mirrors. The source of light is now indeed within the objects, so far as he can tell, and their multiple reflections in the mirror-walls teach him a new assurance: that these objects, bathed in their varied lights and in their reflections, with the possible interrelations among them multiplied by these lights and reflections, are real. Cut off as they are, in all their facets and angles of vision, they are the only reality there is for him, the manifold light the only light. The replicas no longer have their archetypes outside but have become themselves the archetypes. The original "imitation" has taken on the here-ness that transforms it to effigy. He is persuaded of a magical incarnation within these objects.

But the mirrors return to their window function after all, in that he will come to see the world through them again, though this time it is hardly a matter of mere transparency. After the spell has completed itself, he sees the walls as windows once more. But either his eyes or they have altered the nature of what they open upon. Perhaps it is his eyes; if it is the windows, he carries them before his sight from this time forward. When he returns to the world after his stay in the glass house, its familiar objects are newly illuminated for him since he sees in them the more fully visioned objects of the all-reflecting, all-enlightened universe of mirrors which he has left. So now it is the world that seems to be the replica, a shabby replica that needs the illumination from within rather than from without if it is to be fit to live in for this newly sensitized being. But he makes it fit to live in, for he creates it in accordance with his newly awakened capacity for vision. He constructs it anew through the norms of what he now knows its objects must reflect and reveal and shine forth with.[24] He destroys the original (for him) meaningless-ness and vaguely grasped formlessness of these objects to order them as meaningful and fully formed. In creating systems for them, the systems that make life sane—which is to say humanly livable—he has created for the world his own glass house (though one with borrowed walls that consequently lack the "mirrorizing" power). And from this one he is not likely to escape—not, that is, unless or until the process begins again: and one day, newly dazed, he comes upon a different glass house which, if it can persuade him to see its windows changed to mirrors, works its wondrous transformations upon him which can again make his previous world (the once newly constructed glass house of his own) unfit for him; which can force another reconstruction under its tutelage.

Now all this must be seen as a phenomenological process. We need not proclaim an animistic faith by saying that there is real magic in the house or that worlds and their objects really change. About the house, however, only those

[24] For the historicist, the most important of the objects in their original role as replicas may be literally translated out of my allegory as being commonly formulated and espoused ideologies. More technically, we might speak of other recognizable entities in the poem that lead the worldly reader in by seeming familiar: common elements like words and their accepted meanings, normal syntax, formal conventions passed down by the history of art, logical propositions that promise a single dimension of coherent discourse. All these elements, which begin as what in its broadest sense we could call imitative, must undergo the radical transformation to a total here-ness when the windows close to mirrors and throw them back upon themselves—and upon the reader.

are likely to deny its magic whose dedication to seeing *through* windows keeps them from the requisite fascination with the objects (though this is the sort of charge spiritualists make against those who will not take their seance seriously). About the worlds and their objects changing, how can we finally say whether they really do when we each have grasped our version of them in terms of our own glass houses?

But still the process must be acknowledged as possibly a delusion. We need not worry this problem so long as our concern is phenomenological only. For whatever the positive authenticity of the transformation, this process is what makes the human world and, in an aggregate sense, human culture possible. It is what, from the beginning, we have found in the magical world of immediacy which creates the human forms of vision that enable us to systematize *our* reality so as to handle and—to a limited extent only—to control it. The relation of this world to external reality (whatever that is) is of secondary importance or rather of no importance at all for him whose exclusive interest is in human culture, in human ideology, and their sources in racial and historical vision. For this vision, for a mature existential anthropology, we must become archeologists of the most magical, the most persuasively "mirrorized," glass houses of human history.

II

THE MIRROR

AS WINDOW IN SHAKESPEARE'S

SONNETS

INTRODUCTORY

As I HAVE already suggested, my interest in Shakespeare's *Sonnets* centers on the metaphorical system they develop out of the mirror-window metaphor even as they earn this metaphor through the way in which it functions and has its meaning. My intention, then, if I may be so presumptuous as to assume such a task needs doing, is to perform for the *Sonnets* the sort of service William Butler Yeats performed for his poems in writing *A Vision*. That is, I should like to elicit the total mythology which their series of related and mutually revealing metaphors seems to me implicitly to construct.

This intention may seem to be in conflict with my contextualist concern with unique poems, in its opposition to Northrop Frye's more universalistic concern with poetry as a collective body. For if the single sonnet (or, at most, the series of two or three obviously mutually dependent sonnets that form a single 28-line or 42-line poem) should constitute the aesthetic unit, the enclosed set of mirrors, then how can I so open it outward as to make the entire sequence the aesthetic unit? The answer lies in Shakespeare's brilliant method of creating constitutive symbols in one sonnet and, having earned his right to them there, transferring them whole to another sonnet, with their full burden of borrowed meaning, earned elsewhere, taken for granted. Thus a creative symbol in one sonnet becomes a sign, part of the raw materials, in another. An "insistent" metaphor in one sonnet is used as its "existent" equivalent in a second in a way that contributes to a larger "insistent" meaning in the latter. The critic can treat the single poem as an aesthetic unit while still using it as an explicative instrument to reveal the interrelation among the sonnets that creates the oneness of their total symbolic system, their unified body of metaphor. So my contextual treatment of individual sonnets should lead me inevitably toward a metaphorical gloss for the sequence. If this procedure works, then, far from being contradicted, my contextualist argument concerning "insistence" and "existence" should be strongly corroborated.

This is not to claim that all the sonnets are here judged as aesthetically successful. Many of them, of course, are—notably those that earn the fullness of symbol through the metaphorical extension that ends in incarnation. Others that may be less creative are included since these can reveal with what fullness the symbols can function elsewhere in the system, outside their original sonnets, as signs, even though the less successful poem under consideration may not have constructed its own mirrorized walls out of this extramural material. And this demonstration also serves my purpose.

Nor, of course, am I trying to treat the *Sonnets* exhaustively. I do not mean to account for every sonnet or even to touch every sonnet whose relevance to the total system could be shown. With my governing interest in constructing the metaphorical system and proving the creativity of metaphor in single sonnets, I must bring in the sonnets I need as I need them, with my procedure directed by the dialectic of my network of explication rather than by any more ambitious desire to offer a definitive treatment of the *Sonnets*. I should be most gratified if the reader can extend the mythological framework to other sonnets in the sequence since such an extension would confirm the value of this undertaking. In my most optimistic moments I like to think that all the sonnets can be embraced by the total mythology I claim to find. But I must maintain that the theoretical value of this work would remain whether or not they can be so embraced.

But, despite its uniqueness, the individual sonnet is indebted to more than the sequence for its meaning; it is indebted also to the Petrarchan convention that is largely formative of them all and of their innumerable fellows written by Shakespeare's predecessors and contemporaries. In-

deed, that mirror-window image which I find so central is itself drawn from this convention and from the Courtly Love
convention on which it rests.

The problems are almost insurmountable for the Petrarchan sonneteer who comes along as late as Shakespeare and
who wants to be more than conventional. From verse form
to conceits and even attitudes and judgments, there seems to
be almost too much that is dictated by convention for the
uniqueness of individual talent and individual intention to
be given free enough play to create really new poems. So
many extramural commonplaces intrude upon the poem that
it seems almost too much to expect the poem to manage to
close itself up within its own set of enclosed mirror-walls.
But I have been saying "almost" since obviously at his best
Shakespeare does manage to transcend the conventions and
make them his own even as they become the very elements
that give his poems—and his sequence—the "body" that
creates their self-sufficient integrity.

In effect, Shakespeare solves the problem posed by his stale
convention as his persona does in Sonnet 23.

> As an unperfect actor on the stage
> Who with his fear is put besides his part,
> Or some fierce thing replete with too much rage,
> Whose strength's abundance weakens his own heart;
> So I , for fear of trust, forget to say
> The perfect ceremony of love's rite,
> And in mine own love's strength seem to decay,
> O'ercharg'd with burthen of mine own love's might.

The speaker forgets to say "the perfect ceremony of love's
rite" for fear of his not being believed. But what is the
"perfect ceremony," the set part of the "actor on the stage,"
except those conventions that Petrarchism has imposed
through its bearded, if no longer vital, authority upon those
who still would play the lover's (and poet's) role? The poet

loves too deeply ("mine own love's strength," "O'ercharg'd
with burthen of mine own love's might") to abide by the
"perfect ceremony" since his fear of being distrusted (the
"fear of trust," line 5, that is an echo and further specifica-
tion of the "fear" of line 2) leads him, as Petrarchan actor,
to be "unperfect," to forget his lines, because of his very sincerity. This is Shakespeare's answer to the obvious problem
for the Petrarchan: how to protest persuasively that one is
sincere as he uses the instrument that has served so many
others, both sincere and conventionally insincere?

How differently Spenser, much less restive within his convention, treats this problem in his *Amoretti* 54; or rather how
oblivious he shows himself to its very existence.

> Of this world's Theatre in which we stay,
>> My love like the Spectator idly sits
>> beholding me that all the pageants play,
>> disguising diversely my troubled wits.
> Sometimes I joy when glad occasion fits,
>> and mask in mirth like to a Comedy:
>> soon after when my joy to sorrow flits,
>> I wail and make my woes a Tragedy.
> Yet she beholding me with constant eye,
>> delights not in my mirth nor rues my smart:
>> but when I laugh she mocks, and when I cry
>> she laughs, and hardens evermore her heart.
> What then can move her? if nor mirth nor moan,
>> she is no woman, but a senseless stone.[1]

Here the speaker accepts his role as conventional actor, playing and "disguising" before his mistress, wailing and making
his "woes a Tragedy"; and he dares be angry with her for not
responding to his performance as if it were truly felt, for

[1] Here and elsewhere, as editors have done with Shakespeare in the
sonnets I quote, I have modernized Spenser's spellings insofar as I
could do so without in any way changing his language.

not playing the game of make-believe (or is not her disdain precisely appropriate to the role of Petrarchan mistress that she must play to match his role of ardent, suffering Petrarchan lover—and just as conventional an action as his, for just as conventional a role?). We cannot help but see her as a perspicacious figure and him as a naively foolish and unreasonable one.

Shakespeare's lover, in his dual awareness of self and of his role, rejects the so often rehearsed perfection that is by now so unpersuasive. In the sestet of Sonnet 23 he turns from Petrarchan speech to the silence of loving "looks" to convey the depth of his love.

> O, let my looks be then the eloquence
> And dumb presagers of my speaking breast,
> Who plead for love, and look for recompense,
> More than that tongue that more hath more express'd.
>   O, learn to read what silent love hath writ!
>   To hear with eyes belongs to love's fine wit.

It is most surprising and disappointing that some editors still suggest "books" instead of "looks" in the first line quoted. Not only are "books" not commonly used in the sense of poems or verse, but the total force of the sonnet, in its choice of love's silent speech (that is, loving looks) over open protestations of love, would be destroyed since "books," as love poems, would still be forms of rehearsed speech—indeed the only way the Petrarchan poet-lover is allowed to talk. Moreover, in choosing "looks" as love's silent speech, Shakespeare's speaker is also choosing a conventionally Petrarchan alternative. Like any convention that has staying power, Petrarchism must have a built-in skepticism against itself. The protesting against playing the conventional role, the impatience with the lover's complaints, leads to the silent speech of eyes and heart as an equally conventional reaction to the normal Petrarchan action. (For example, see also

Spencer's *Amoretti* 43, "Shall I then silent be or shall I speak?" in which the poet-lover is in trouble with his mistress if he speaks, in trouble with his own stifled emotions if he does not, and so chooses to teach his "heart" and "eyes" "with silence secretly" to speak.) Sonnet 23 thus is in effect written against the writing of the sonnet as an outlet for plaintive speech. And the convention has furnished its own, almost equally conventional, antithesis.

Of course, Shakespeare, in Sonnet 23, goes far beyond the convention in his recognition of the inadequacy of the conventional role in the face of the surge of strong personal emotion. The conflict between the actor and the "fierce thing," the conflict between weakness and strength that changes from conflict to a definition of weakness as too much strength—these lead to the notion of imperfection as excess through an over-burdening of the very emotion necessary to initiate the poems. All these make the Petrarchan Shakespeare's wrestling with his convention—in language as well as concept—uniquely his own struggle. And so is his resolution his own, as anti-Petrarchism is reconciled to the tradition after all. As we shall see again and again in the *Sonnets*, this is Shakespeare's way of making his claim while showing us the difficulty, even the impossibility, of making it. Is not his final irony here the fact that, despite his argument for love's silent and private speech rather than the perfection of the actor's conventional and public speech (of which the routine Petrarchan sonnet is an example *par excellence*), this argument is made in a poem which is itself hardly silent and is itself an example of this very Petrarchan mode?[2] The argu-

[2] See his Sonnet 130 ("My mistress' eyes are nothing like the sun") for a more obvious—in my opinion a too obvious—example of anti-Petrarchan Petrarchism, as he closes with the Petrarchan hyperbolic insistence on the beloved's unsurpassed beauty after scornfully denying the usual Petrarchan attributes. The force of his couplet here ("And yet, by heaven, I think my love as rare / As any she belied with false compare") simply enlarges the group of those to whom Petrarchan praises should

ment against the conventional poetic outcry is made in a conventional poem, its own best demonstration against the claim it argues for so ably. For in using the convention he denies, Shakespeare proves how fresh, how new, it can be made, how it can be put in the service of the very emotional strength that—in the weakness of that strength—sought to undo it.

In his conflict with his tradition throughout the sequence, then, we must be thankful Shakespeare chose not the alternative of silence but the alternative of his own speech, of a verbal mastery that turned the convention into a traditional poetry that is ever self-renewed.

---

be applicable, despite his seeming dismissal of the usual catalogue of Petrarchan praises. But in its playfulness Sonnet 130 is not, in the sense in which Sonnet 23 is, a poem fully serious in its addressing of the poet's conflict with his convention.

1. THE MIRROR OF
NARCISSUS AND THE MAGICAL
MIRROR OF LOVE

Mine eye hath play'd the painter and hath stell'd
Thy beauty's form in table of my heart;
My body is the frame wherein 'tis held,
And perspective it is best painter's art.
For through the painter must you see his skill
To find where your true image pictur'd lies;
Which in my bosom's shop is hanging still,
That hath his windows glazed with thine eyes.

The octave of Sonnet 24 presents just the relation between mirror and window that has been concerning me. This relation arises out of the common Petrarchan conceit—originally borrowed from medieval physiology—which allows the eye to appropriate its object in beholding it, or, if I may justify the pun, in apprehending it. The Petrarchan lover, of course, spiritualizes this appropriation, the form of the beloved residing in his heart. How can the beloved find proof that she exists in her lover?[1] By looking into the eyes of the poet, seeing in them her image as in a distorted mirror. But what she sees is not a mere reflection; the conceit, rather, must fancifully maintain that in looking into the eyes she sees through a window to the poet's heart in which her form is

[1] Where I speak of Petrarchan sonnets generically, as I do here, I may use the feminine in referring to the beloved although most of the Shakespearean sonnets I shall speak about are probably addressed to a man. It is just too convenient for me to resist the ease of reference allowed by using contrasting genders where I can in referring to poet-lover and beloved. Nor do I intend to try to argue that Shakespeare's 1–126 were or were not all addressed to one person or to persons of one sex. In view of the chaste character of the neo-Platonic love he speaks of—like that in The Phoenix and Turtle—I must maintain that, whatever the truth, my case would not be altered by it. Thus I shall speak of the poet's beloved friend as the object of all of them alike.

lodged. The mirror has become window; reflection which seems to return one upon oneself suddenly is transformed to transparence which opens outward into the soul of the lover.[2]

Thus the image captured in the eyes (or rather, to take the conceit seriously, through the eyes in the heart) is a very special one, indeed totally unique: the very essence of the beloved which only the lover can permit her to perceive. Of course, if we leave the figurative level of the conceit, at the level of the tenor all we have is the doubtful commonplace that the eyes of love see profoundly and truly, creating an image that is the reality. But for me—and, if I am right, for these poets—the significance goes far beyond the prose paraphrase. They, and we, must be more gullible. We must be prepared to take a preposition like "through" in line 5 of Shakespeare's Sonnet 24 quite seriously: "through the painter" means not merely by means of the painter but literally *through* him. For the painter has been identified with the eye, and it is through the eye and *only* through the eye that the beloved can be humanly reflected in a way that turns the ap-

[2] Later we shall see that this conceit will help establish the neo-Platonic unity between the lovers—in analogy to the Christian Trinity —so necessary to the claim of substantial oneness. Compare with the totality of substantive transfer in this passage and others to be examined the rather flat, straightforward claim of Sonnet 22 (in the second quatrain) which, for all its similarity to this one, is but an unearned postulation:

> My glass shall not persuade me I am old
> So long as youth and thou are of one date;
> But when in thee time's furrows I behold,
> Then look I death my days should expiate.
> For all that beauty that doth cover thee
> Is but the seemly raiment of my heart,
> Which in thy breast doth live, as thine in me.
> How can I then be elder than thou art?

Here we have only the poet's word for it, reinforced of course by his other, more creative sonnets and by the habits of his inherited convention which he here does not transcend. For, unlike others, this poem has not made the claim good on its own. Its claim remains merely "poetic"— which is to say extravagant—without being made into a poem.

pearance into the "true image." So, as the conceit would have it, the image is seen not just *in* the eye-as-painter but *through* the eye-as-painter. The eye becomes the one indispensable place in which (and through which) the image can be true. Unlike other reflecting agents, the eye of the Petrarchan lover is the unique locus of the true image. It cannot be transferred or translated, for only here the mirror opens outward to be window too. The enclosure of self-love is broken by love. It is precisely this movement to total identity in the metaphor —to the union of the *in* and the *through*—that characterizes these sonnets and the theory I have been constructing that runs parallel to them.

What gives even more strength to the image in Sonnet 24, and to our need to take it seriously,[3] is the sestet of Sonnet 23. Here in a proper Petrarchan manner, the poet's "looks" are summoned to plead his love and his beloved summoned to hear this silent speech (of the eyes) with his own eyes. Sonnet 24 relates the consequence of this mutual confrontation of the eyes of lovers. They are not returned upon themselves but enter each other, proving their unity in a substantial, incarnating way that becomes the spiritualized, neo-Platonic equivalent of the sexual union.[4]

An awareness of the implications of this conceit would help us make total sense of Sonnet 45 of Edmund Spenser's

---

[3] I have more than once now used this evasive adverb, "seriously," probably because in speaking of figures of speech I am embarrassed to say "literally," really the word I mean. From here on I shall manage the courage to use it of those moments in which, as John Crowe Ransom says, poems have the courage of their metaphors. For my entire claim will be lost if metaphors are not seen as literal rather than just figurative entities.

[4] Let me confess to being totally baffled by the couplet of Sonnet 24, which, in its derogation of the eyes and its distinction between eye and heart, runs counter to all that precedes. It is as if Shakespeare—perhaps diverted by the epigrammatic needs of the couplet—has retreated from his conceit, from applying full pressure to the substantive transfer of properties that is embodied in it.

Amoretti, in which the same confrontation is appealed to. This poem in turn can help clarify the possibilities in the conceit by revealing how literally it can be extended. The poem normally seems difficult because there is an ellipsis which those familiar with Petrarchism, as were Spenser's intended readers, might well be expected to fill in.

> Leave lady in your glass of crystal clean,
>> Your goodly self for evermore to view:
>> and in my self, my inward self I mean,
>> most lively like behold your semblant true.
> Within my heart, though hardly it can show
>> thing so divine to view of earthly eye,
>> the fair Idea of your celestial hue,
>> and every part remains immortally:
> And were it not that through your cruelty,
>> with sorrow dimmed and deform'd it were:
>> the goodly image of your visnomy,
>> clearer than crystal would therein appear.
> But if your self in me ye plain will see,
>> remove the cause by which your fair beams darken'd be.

Here the lady is being called away from the merely reflective vanity of the looking-glass to view in the poet an image that is more than what Plato would term mere appearance; it is her "semblant true," her "fair Idea" because it is what love has unerringly made of her. So it is far beyond mere physical reflection. Yet how is she to have access to the poet's heart which, as usual, is the home of the image? If the metaphor is to have any meaning on the literal level of the vehicle, clearly she must find a way in. Just as clearly, from the Petrarchan convention and from the rest of the poem, it must be through the poet's eyes that she can gain admission to the heart. Again this must be the substantive base for this airy claim. To begin with, it is likely that the lady is being asked to exchange her mirror for something in some ways similar in function. We must note that the "glass of crystal clean," which she is asked to forego, will be surpassed by that which would yield a "goodly image" "clearer than crystal" if she would but cooperate. For because of her cruelty the image in his heart is now "with sorrow dimmed and deform'd." Is it too much for us to see here a witty reference to the tears caused in his eyes by her which dim and deform the new mirror that, seeming to give her back an image, is really the window to his heart? This is indeed an indispensable reading, and I feel we must supply it from the convention.

What she is called upon to see in the second glass, for which she is to give up her "glass of crystal clean," is not, of course, just her reflection. For in this case she would merely be returned upon herself, still trapped by mere appearance; and for mere appearance she cannot do better than the "crystal clean."[5] The eyes, in becoming windows, allow her to go beyond mere appearance and beyond her self-containment. They lead her outward to the heart of love and the spiritual truth, the "fair Idea" found there, the truth that true love bestows upon fleshly reality. But still the only way in is by way of the eyes; and the dimming, deforming, and darkening of the image there has, in terms of the conceit, obvious, immediate, and fearful consequences on the transcendent reality in the heart. This reality is after all dependent on accidents in the flesh! Just the price of a truly substantive metaphor. For after all, the literal level of the metaphor—which must get her to the heart only by way of the eyes—insists that in becoming windows to the heart the eyes still never stop functioning as the mirror into which she looks once she has given up her more limited mirror of "crystal clean."

[5] This unmagical mirror, the "glass of crystal clean," performs its function within an epistemology that asserts an unrefracted window-reality and thus serves as what, in this essay, I would term *mere* window, as I tried to make clear in footnote 2, p. 3, where I equate the mirror of simple *mimesis* with the window-function of language.

Any "apparent" dimming or deformity of the image in the eye is a real deformity in what is carried in the heart. The level of appearance is not abandoned after all in the attainment of more-than-appearance since the action of the poem insists on, depends on, just this level. The poet manages to have it both ways! Surely it must be to the lady's advantage, then, to keep this new mirror clear since its window-function is so inseparable from its mirror-function. It must indeed be "clearer" (literally more clairvoyant) than "crystal" (line 12)—and thus the witty insistence that she mend her ways toward him, for her sake.

Shakespeare has from the start of his sonnet sequence depended on the substantive transfer embodied in the eye-image that becomes reality. The first seventeen sonnets, in which he in various ways exhorts his friend to marry and breed, have been underrated, in part because of the lack of variation in the prose meaning, but—more important—in part because of our failure to see the infinitely varied ramifications of the image of the eye as mirror and window. In this group, of course, it is the child who takes the place of the poet-lover as the reflecting and incarnating agent. Two magnificent stanzas from *The Rape of Lucrece*, when old Lucretius laments his dead daughter, present the pattern most tellingly:

"Daughter, dear daughter!" old Lucretius cries,
"That life was mine which thou hast here deprived.
If in the child the father's image lies,
Where shall I live now Lucrece is unlived?
Thou was not to this end from me derived.
    If children predecease progenitors,
    We are their offspring, and they none of ours.

"Poor broken glass, I often did behold
In thy sweet semblance my old age new born;
But now that fresh fair mirror, dim and old,
Shows me a bare-bon'd death by time outworn.

O, from thy cheeks my image thou hast torn
And shiver'd all the beauty of my glass,
That I no more can see what once I was."

(lines 1751–1764)

She was to be the mirror that unites past and present and guarantees the future. As such she was more than mirror in that she destroyed time by maintaining an eternal present for the aging father, thus defeating that aging. She was his window on the future even as she was his mirror of the past. With her death the magic is fled, so that now all that remains is a frightful mirror that is nothing more than mirror of his own impending death and the end of everything. From her being a vision of his "old age new born," she now—as a mirror suddenly "dim and old"—can reflect only "a bare-bon'd death by time outworn." The "broken glass" is the objective equivalent of the old man's life, broken and ending; the magic looking-glass that enabled him to step into the future is gone:

O, from thy cheeks my image thou hast torn
And shiver'd all the beauty of my glass,
That I no more can see what once I was.

It is just this blessing of parenthood—the projection and extension of self beyond self—that Shakespeare in the opening sonnets calls upon his friend to accept. The language of Sonnet 3 is helpfully similar.

Look in thy glass and tell the face thou viewest
Now is the time that face should form another,
Whose fresh repair if now thou not renewest,
Thou dost beguile the world, unbless some mother.
For where is she so fair whose unear'd womb
Disdains the tillage of thy husbandry?
Or who is he so fond will be the tomb
Of his self-love, to stop posterity?

Thou art thy mother's glass, and she in thee
Calls back the lovely April of her prime.
So thou through windows of thine age shalt see,
Despite of wrinkles, this thy golden time.
But if thou live remember'd not to be,
Die single, and thine image dies with thee.

As in Spenser's Sonnet 45, the poet begins by calling upon his beloved to forego the mirror that flatters vanity in order to discover a reflection that becomes more than just reflective, a reflection that is substantive, in effect an incarnation. Instead of the face watching its apparent reflection, a lifeless insubstantial echo, the poet pleads for it to create a reflection that is progressive, that is itself come again. The word "repair" (line 3) does double service in creating this meaning: however fair the face, the ravages of time will increasingly require its "repair" (that is, its improvement, its revival, even its total restoration), although there is no method of restoration that can defeat time's assault upon beauty except for the "repair" (that is, the coming, the arrival) of a new edition of the face ready to initiate the cycle again.

This sonnet makes our task easy by moving explicitly from mirror to window. The "glass" of line 1 is the simple, unmagical mirror, Spenser's "glass of crystal clean." By line 9 the "glass" has the magical procreative powers we have seen old Lucretius attribute to the child:

Thou art thy mother's glass, and she in thee
Calls back the lovely April of her prime.

This power to reverse history, literally to see through time, makes this glass a window by virtue of its being so remarkable a mirror. Shakespeare has even earned the right to use the word "windows" in the line immediately following:

So thou through windows of thine age shalt see,
Despite of wrinkles, this thy golden time.

But in the couplet, where the poet returns to the friend's unmarried state, he must return also to the prosaic mirror that ruthlessly gives back to us the fickle process of living: "Die single, and thine image dies with thee." A limited, fated image that can do no tricks with time, as the friend is left sharing the tragic estate of Old Lucretius, in the throes of his catastrophe.

This sonnet leads also to another area of metaphor which will allow us to extend the one I have been examining. So often in the "breed" sonnets the plea to the friend is based on the appeal to the natural order. Aside from this one, Sonnets 1, 5, and 12 will be seen to furnish especially impressive testimony. The appeal is understandable enough, since the poet's argument, we have seen, calls for the friend to join the process of generation, of rebirth ("the gaudy spring" of Sonnet 1) that keeps the world ever new, ever repeating itself, even in the face of death. In repeating itself, nature seems to use the mirror on itself, its members and their operations, even as it marches forward through history. History which seems so simply linear is at the same time circular, filled with the eternal return that is yet progressive. For death is not finally denied; indeed, the homely realities of chronology are affirmed as part of the necessary cycle. By now we have learned that this magical manner of at once submitting to and transcending time is the equivalent of the simultaneous operations of mirror as mirror and mirror as window.

So in Sonnet 3 the friend is urged to imitate nature, like Schiller's "naive poet" to join the natural community that eternalizes the individual by communalizing him, by making him one with history. We are reminded of Tennyson's Tithonus, who, wearied of his strange sort of personal immortality, longs only to join the march of common humanity who voluntarily submit to the natural cycles of mortality that together constitute another sort of immortality:

Man comes and tills the field and lies beneath.

Thus the language of Shakespeare's lines 5 and 6:

> For where is she so fair whose unear'd womb
> Disdains the tillage of thy husbandry?

The final word draws together three crucial lines of meaning. First, it has the obvious meaning relevant to the metaphor of farming: his "husbandry," tilling that which was unploughed, will produce the fruit of the future. Secondly, it has the obvious meaning related to marriage: the proper exercise of his functions of "husbandry" will produce his heir. Thus this is the precise word to join the natural and human realms, to insist that his fully human function can be exercised only by the more essential natural function that sanctions it. But there is also a third meaning that transcends and unites the other two: "husbandry" as intelligent, conservative management. For it is only by accepting the need for husbandry in the other senses that the friend can conserve— can keep from expending, exhausting—the great value that is himself. This is the controlling sense of the word, the sense consistent with the charges of the bachelor's wasteful niggarding in Sonnets 1 and 4. By spending himself as husband, he creates himself again in the mirror that is his window; by jealously saving himself from others, he succeeds only in entombing himself and his image for good. In the biblical sense, only those can find themselves who lose themselves, only those can husband themselves who, by husbanding another, give themselves away. This act, proper "husbandry," this totally natural act, can break through time:

> Thou art thy mother's glass, and she in thee
> Calls back the lovely April of her prime.
> So thou through windows of thine age shalt see,
> Despite of wrinkles, this thy golden time.

The "golden time" of course is an allusion to the golden age, the pastoral idyll of eternal gamboling youth—in effect, an eternal "April of [one's] prime." The way of generation, of the identifying of self with natural history (of which, in the pastoral mood, human history is but a reflective part), is the way to earn one's passage into the pastoral Eden. For the window does open onto yet another April, another prime, another golden time, "despite of wrinkles."

It becomes clear that the appeal to imitate the natural order, or rather to acknowledge one's part in it, with its eternal rebirth and its transcendence of singularity, comes by way of turning nature into Eden, by way of the pastoral convention which has always insisted on nature as a reflection of man. We have come to another manipulation of the mirror-image —or is it just another angle of the original one, with man called upon to move outward, to use procreative nature, rather than his enclosed narcissistic self, as his mirror? Again we can turn to Spenser for a helpful demonstration, this time to two stanzas (lines 19–30) from the January eclogue of *The Shepherd's Calendar:*

> Thou barren ground, whom winters wrath hath wasted,
> Art made a mirror, to behold my plight:
> Whilom thy fresh spring flower'd, and after hasted
> Thy summer proud with Daffadillies dight.
> And now is come thy winters stormy state,
> Thy mantle mard, wherein thou maskedst late.
>
> Such rage as winter's, reigneth in my heart,
> My life blood freezing with unkindly cold:
> Such stormy stoures do breed my baleful smart,
> As if my year were waste, and woxen old.
> And yet alas, but now my spring begun,
> And yet alas, it is already done.

Nature as the mirror of man, the cycle of nature's year as the cycle of man's life. These lines are spoken by the young

Colin Clout, with his year and his life ahead, who already foresees their end. Happily for Spenser's purpose, the year begins in January and ends in December, moving from bleakness to bleakness.[6] The December eclogue, spoken by the aging Colin, is a mere echo of the January eclogue. All of December has been foreseen in January by the youthful Colin, whose end is indeed in his beginning:

> Such rage as winter's, reigneth in my heart,
> My life blood freezing with unkindly cold:
> Such stormy stoures do breed my baleful smart,
> As if my year were waste, and woxen old.
> And yet alas, but now my spring begun,
> And yet alas, it is already done.

For the year's end (winter) is also its beginning (winter), and the pastoral has man's life as a reflection of nature's. Here is the circular concept indeed.

The equating of man's life to nature's year is of course quite traditional. Spenser makes the equation work by his relativistic use of the word "year." Remember Colin's "As if my year were waste, and woxen old." And in December the pastoral hero, now indeed old, nearing an end that he in effect forelived at the beginning in January, echoes:

> So now my year draws to his latter term,
> My spring is spent, my summer burnt up quite:
> My harvest hastes to stir up winter stern,
> And bids him claim with rigorous rage his right.
>   (December, lines 127–130)

[6] In the "argument" prefatory to *The Shepherd's Calendar*, E. K., the supposed editor, apologizes for Spenser's starting in January instead of March, "when the sonne reneweth his finished course, and the seasonable spring refresheth the earth, and the plesaunce thereof being buried in the sadnesse of the dead winter now worne away, reliveth." But my point is that it is precisely suited to Spenser's need for circularity to have his first eclogue as similar as possible to his last and that it was thus far more useful to begin in January than in the more dramatic resurgence of March.

A year, then, is the term of any single life-cycle, the astronomical "sphere" of any person or planet. Spenser's brilliant and witty Sonnet 60, built entirely on the conflicts among the seemingly varying lengths of years, begins by presenting this linguistically tricky notion most lucidly:

> They that in course of heavenly spheres are skill'd,
> To every planet point his sundry year:
> In which her circle's voyage is fulfill'd,
> As Mars in three score years doth run his sphere.

We must note that the "year" of line 2 is the relativistic concept, varying with the cycle of each differing subject, while ironically the "years" of line 4 refer to our earth-bound year (in the poem one-sixtieth the "year" of Mars). But, as Shakespeare does in his Sonnet 59, we must wonder "whether revolution be the same." Despite differences of seeming, a year's a year—or a life-cycle a life-cycle—for all that. The circular concept both destroys normal time and creates mirrors among the cycles. As a natural concept it ties man to nature, promising him freedom from time's yoke if he surrenders himself and his singularity to the natural community —if he merges with history.

But besides the extraordinary, repetitive powers of natural circularity, there is the alternative mirror: the unmagical mirror we have seen that returns upon itself, comes to an end in itself, the minute finitude of total egocentricity. This is the mirror that allowed the final line of Sonnet 3, "Die single, and thine image dies with thee." Clearly this is the mirror of Narcissus and is equally the instrument of self-love. The Narcissus story itself is mentioned, not in the "breed" sonnets, but in the similar argument advanced by Venus—in a kind of parody of these sonnets—in the approximately contemporary *Venus and Adonis*.[7] In a context all too similar

[7] It may seem to undercut Shakespeare's sincerity in his Sonnets 1–17 to find that Venus, often using language and imagery much like Shake-

to that of the opening sonnets, Venus explicitly relates Narcissus to the argument against self-love:

> "Is thine own heart to thine own face affected?
> Can thy right hand seize love upon thy left?
> Then woo thyself, be of thyself rejected;
> Steal thine own freedom, and complain on theft.
> Narcissus so himself himself forsook,
> And died to kiss his shadow in the brook."
>
> (lines 157–162)

Without an explicit Narcissus, we have seen him lurking behind the lines of Sonnet 3; he is implicitly even more involved in Sonnets 1 and 4:

> From fairest creatures we desire increase,
> That thereby beauty's rose might never die,
> But as the riper should by time decease,
> His tender heir might bear his memory;
> But thou, contracted to thine own bright eyes,
> Feed'st thy light's flame with self-substantial fuel,
> Making a famine where abundance lies,
> Thyself thy foe, to thy sweet self too cruel.
> Thou that art now the world's fresh ornament
> And only herald to the gaudy spring,

---

speare's to his friend, attempts to seduce Adonis with precisely this insistence on the need to breed (see lines 127–132, 157–174, 751–768). We should remember, however, that the questionable use to which Venus puts this argument does not necessarily indicate that Shakespeare did not hold the argument itself to be valid. Indeed, may not the most serious charge against Venus be her use of sound argument for unsound purposes? Adonis says as much—and testifies to the intrinsic worth of her argument—when he answers her pleas for his multiplying himself:

> I hate not love, but your device in love,
> That lends embracements unto every stranger.
> You do it for increase. O strange excuse,
> When reason is the bawd to lust's abuse!
>
> (lines 789–792)

Within thine own bud buriest thy content
And, tender churl, mak'st waste in niggarding.
  Pity the world, or else this glutton be,
  To eat the world's due, by the grave and thee.

Unthrifty loveliness, why dost thou spend
Upon thyself thy beauty's legacy?
Nature's bequest gives nothing, but doth lend,
And, being frank, she lends to those are free.
Then, beauteous niggard, why dost thou abuse
The bounteous largess given thee to give?
Profitless usurer, why dost thou use
So great a sum of sums, yet canst not live?
For, having traffic with thyself alone,
Thou of thyself thy sweet self dost deceive.
Then how, when nature calls thee to be gone,
What acceptable audit canst thou leave?
  Thy unus'd beauty must be tomb'd with thee,
  Which, used, lives th' executor to be.

As Venus is with Adonis, the poet can be quite violent in
his charges of narcissism. The self-love is insisted upon quite
graphically, in language that, beginning in natural beauty,
comes to be related to appetite—even to sexual appetite—and
to crass finance. After the idyllic first quatrain of Sonnet 1, the
poet forcefully sets the contrast with the double-edged "contracted." Primarily, of course, the word refers to the mar-
riage-contract of the friend with himself, the culmination—
indeed the consummation—of self-love proclaimed by the
"self-substantial fuel" of the next line and reinforced by line
11 ("Within thine own bud buriest thy content"). By Sonnet
4 the tone of derogation has increased to the bitterness of
"having traffic with thyself alone." But self-marriage has a
consequence that brings us to the other and yet more con-
sequential meaning of "contracted." By so restricting his
human intercourse to his traffic with himself, the friend con-

tracts—that is, shrinks—the world to himself. The egocentric predicament is complete. By being married to his own eyes, his world is reduced to his own eyes. Instead of looking into the eyes of a beloved and having a mirror that can open outward by being transformed to a window, instead of looking at the product of such love—a son who is himself both mirror and window, both repetition and progression, a second coming—he can look only into the unmagical mirror that shows him his own eyes, into Spenser's "glass of crystal clean." His own eyes can reflect only the self that ages, the reflection and the self coming to an end together. This word "contracted" cannot help reminding us of the use of the same word and same image applied to the true lovers who have escaped into each other in John Donne's *The Canonization:*

> Who did the whole world's soul contract, and drove
>   Into the glasses of your eyes—
>   So made such mirrors and such spies
> That they did all to you epitomize . . .

Quite a different marriage, this more inclusive contract that creates a world. This is the marriage that Shakespeare is desperately calling for.

It is the narcissistic mode of contracting which leads to the self-deprivation that converts self-love to self-hate. And it is self-love as self-hate (as well, of course, as the obvious hate of others) that sets going the series of paradoxes that follow (famine and abundance in line 7, foe and sweet self in line 8, "tender churl" and "mak'st waste in niggarding" in line 12). This series leads to the major play—in language of the marketplace—on "use," "abuse," "unused," and "usury" in Sonnets 4, 6, and 9. For having a contract with one's eyes and having one's world contracted to one's eyes—both essentially the same contracting act and thus deserving of the one word—are ways not only of depriving love and life of their natural rights, but also of making time and death the total destroyers of all one is and has ("Die single, and thine image dies with thee"). For one's own eyes, all that one is restricted to in the "glass of crystal clean," have no historical dimension to keep them from closing utterly, from being their own tomb. Thus the self-destruction, without any Phoenix-like resurrection, of line 6 ("Feed'st thy light's flame with self-substantial fuel") and the self-tombing implied by the verb of line 11 ("Within thine own bud buriest thy content"). Finally, in the last line ("To eat the world's due, by the grave and thee"), the language of the blind, irrepressible, niggardly glutton reveals the friend not only as a collaborator of death but as one who anticipates death by doing the worm's destructive work on this side of the tomb.

This notion returns us to the friend as himself "the tomb / Of his self-love" in Sonnet 3. Here Shakespeare multiplies his effectiveness by rhyming "tomb" with "womb." The opposition is total and the alternatives absolute: love, the womb, the life of an ever-returning April; or self-love, the tomb, the death that closes in after an April that comes only once. Similarly, the word "prime," in the momentary perfection it suggests, and especially in its rhyming relation not just to "time" but to the "golden time," further complicates the meeting between linear and circular time, between life passing and eternal recurrence. It is the recognition of the full significance of "womb" as an antagonistic analogue of "tomb" and of the ambiguous relations between "prime" and "golden time" that justifies the shift from the "glass" of line 1 to the transitional "glass" of line 9 that leads to "windows" in line 11. The miracle, we have seen, is the totally natural one of regeneration. It is what brought the union among the several senses of "husbandry" which we examined earlier. For the ministering to the need of the land to flower is, from the perspective of these poems, identical with the ministering to the human need to multiply its Aprils. The social-historical function is but an aspect of the universal natural function, and the latter is served by husbandry in the broadest sense, the husbanding of the energies of life and April, and with it the denial of the closedness (of the very closet) of the tomb for the infinite flow of an open history out of the womb.

But the poet, in his celebration of nature's circle, does not blink the end of the individual's linear time. The return of April after winter, of the day after the night, occurs in the acknowledgment of all that the end of the daily cycle or of the yearly cycle destroys. Sonnet 12 brilliantly balances the loss with the hope of salvage in an even greater balance of the natural and the human—or rather in the union between them:

> When I do count the clock that tells the time
> And see the brave day sunk in hideous night,
> When I behold the violet past prime
> And sable curls all silver'd o'er with white,
> When lofty trees I see barren of leaves,
> Which erst from heat did canopy the herd,
> And summer's green all girded up in sheaves
> Borne on the bier with white and bristly beard—
> Then of thy beauty do I question make
> That thou among the wastes of time must go,
> Since sweets and beauties do themselves forsake
> And die as fast as they see others grow,
> > And nothing 'gainst Time's scythe can make defence
> > Save breed, to brave him when he takes thee hence.

In the octave the poet, in two-line units, looks at various evidences of time's passage. After the initial general statement, he juxtaposes the faded violet with the faded hair. Then with the "barren" trees which in their fruitful days had protected "the herd," nature is brought into explicit relation with animal life, since here the two, trees and herd, are more than analogous coordinates, as were violet and curls.

97

Or is the herd human too by extension, humanity in its natural—its communal, its herd—aspect? And is this not the herd which *is* under nature's protection, the nature in whose fruitfulness, mirror of its own, it must trust? The union is made total—that is, substantive—in lines 7–8: there is the implied funeral of "summer's green" which as we watch is transformed from simple personification to a literal funeral. It is, of course, the "bier" and its crucial echo in "beard" which manage this utter transformation. Unquestionably "beard" is brilliant: in its vegetative meaning it is true to the now lifeless "green," even as, in combination with the almost homonymous "bier" which makes it possible for "beard" to work, it humanizes the ritual procession.

In three two-line units we have moved from analogy to relation to identity. Although this poem, as one of Shakespeare's "when . . . when . . . then" sonnets, seems to promise only a series of undeveloped, alternative analogies drawn from an apparently random association and designed to illustrate a single general claim, it has gradually grown into a full, total, and even substantive union of its varied elements. The same, seemingly random movement from chance analogy to the two-faced, single-bodied metaphor may be seen in all but the couplets of Sonnets 73 and 60. In these also we can only marvel at the developing interchange of properties between the natural and the human as we watch it become total. I shall not take the space to do more than quote, though we could trace the development as successfully as in Sonnet 12.

> That time of year thou mayst in me behold
> When yellow leaves, or none, or few, do hang
> Upon those boughs which shake against the cold,
> Bare ruin'd choirs where late the sweet birds sang.
> In me thou see'st the twilight of such day
> As after sunset fadeth in the West,
> Which by-and-by black night doth take away,

Death's second self, that seals up all in rest.
In me thou see'st the glowing of such fire
That on the ashes of his youth doth lie,
As the deathbed whereon it must expire,
Consum'd with that which it was nourish'd by.

Or from the magnificent 60:

Like as the waves make towards the pebbled shore,
So do our minutes hasten to their end;
Each changing place with that which goes before,
In sequent toil all forwards do contend.
Nativity, once in the main of light,
Crawls to maturity, wherewith being crown'd,
Crooked eclipses 'gainst his glory fight,
And Time that gave doth now his gift confound.
Time doth transfix the flourish set on youth
And delves the parallels in beauty's brow,
Feeds on the rarities of nature's truth,
And nothing stands but for his scythe to mow.[8]

We have seen in Sonnet 12 that we have not left the natural level, though we have gained the human. We have done it by seeing the human reduced to the natural terms which have now, by extension, become human as well. It is the human *sub specie naturae,* the human that has earned its way to the poet's language. In Sonnet 12 it is the summer's green that has been cut down, as well as its "beard," that justifies on the literal level the use of "Time's scythe" which cuts several ways by cutting its one universal way in line 13. Time as the reaper with scythe or sickle is common enough in these sonnets, as it is everywhere, but Shakespeare here makes it justly this sonnet's.

[8] Perhaps the most brilliant of examples of the human-natural merger occurs in that most successful "When . . . when" sonnet, "When I have seen by Time's fell hand defaced" (Sonnet 64), which I do not quote here since it is to be extensively discussed in a later context.

But in the couplet of Sonnet 12 nature also points the way to resurrection, the universal way that is the way of "breed," always the answer to the "barren," the always newly won "canopy" for "the herd." In terms of the sonnet, it is the "brave" way. We recall that in line 2 it was the *"brave* day" that was lost as symbol for all that time destroys. This phrase reasserts itself in the "brave" of the last line ("Save breed, to brave him when he takes thee hence"). In this line "brave" is an echo, a reflection of the "breed" with which it alliterates: it is the breeding which is the braving of time. But as an echo also of line 2, "brave" is at the same time a kind of equivalent for day, that which the "hideous night" has replaced. By braving time through breed, the friend in effect restores the bravery which is day, overcoming night which is hideous in that it is the end of things. Language again functions as the magical mirror of itself which it is, a mirror magical in the same way as the mirror of breed promises to be. For in the last line "breed" breeds the act of braving time which is a return of the "brave day" which time, except for breed (and its consequent rebraving), had obliterated.

The "brave state" of Sonnet 15 (line 8) is a strengthened version of the "lovely April" of one's "prime," thanks to the accretions of meaning that trail "brave" from Sonnet 12. Sonnets 15, 16, and 17 form a single 42-line unit in which the human and the natural are seemingly in conflict, except that there is a total resolution between them that approaches the kind of union we have several times seen.

> When I consider every thing that grows
> Holds in perfection but a little moment,
> That this huge stage presenteth naught but shows
> Whereon the stars in secret influence comment;
> When I perceive that men as plants increase,
> Cheered and check'd even by the selfsame sky,

Vaunt in their youthful sap, at height decrease,
And wear their brave state out of memory:
Then the conceit of this inconstant stay
Sets you most rich in youth before my sight,
Where wasteful Time debateth with Decay
To change your day of youth to sullied night.
    And, all in war with Time for love of you,
    As he takes from you, I ingraft you new.

But wherefore do not you a mightier way
Make war upon this bloody tyrant, Time?
And fortify yourself in your decay
With means more blessed than my barren rhyme?
Now stand you on the top of happy hours;
And many maiden gardens, yet unset,
With virtuous wish would bear your living flowers,
Much liker than your painted counterfeit.
So should the lines of life that life repair
Which this time's pencil, or my pupil pen,
Neither in inward worth nor outward fair
Can make you live yourself in eyes of men.
    To give away yourself keeps yourself still,
    And you must live, drawn by your own sweet skill.

Who will believe my verse in time to come
If it were fill'd with your most high deserts?
Though yet, heaven knows, it is but as a tomb
Which hides your life and shows not half your parts.
If I could write the beauty of your eyes
And in fresh numbers number all your graces,
The age to come would say, "This poet lies!
Such heavenly touches ne'er touch'd earthly faces."
So should my papers (yellowed with their age)
Be scorn'd, like old men of less truth than tongue,
And your true rights be term'd a poet's rage

And stretched metre of an antique song.
But were some child of yours alive that time,
You should live twice—in it, and in my rhyme.

The three sonnets form an obvious dialectic of thesis, antithesis, and synthesis, respectively. Sonnet 15, another deceptive "when . . . when . . . then" poem, is the first sonnet of the sequence to suggest an alternative answer to breed. The problem of age and death is to be solved not by nature and reproduction but by man and his art. But the suggestion is momentary, since it is withdrawn in Sonnet 16 to allow for breed, nature's solution, once more; and it emerges again in Sonnet 17 only in connection with breed and probably in subjugation to it.

The attempt in Sonnet 15 to brave time by human and artful, as opposed to natural, means is doomed by the very manner in which the challenge of time is posited. For the challenge is universal and surely includes man in the universal reduction to "the fools of time" (to use the language of a later sonnet). The "every thing" of the first line permits of no exceptions. Indeed, it is time that ties man to nature as it subjects all equally to its ruthless law. The all-inclusiveness, the total leveling, in the sonnet is impressive. It reminds us that the "when . . . when . . . then" poem, as we saw with Sonnet 12, moves in its seemingly random way from example to example in part to show the unrestricted universality of the process: wherever the poet turns he sees it similarly at work. Thus the "every thing" finds its echo in the unqualified "naught but" of line 3, the "selfsame" of line 6; and as a most constant "conceit" it sharply underlines the "inconstant stay" (line 9) which characterizes man's feeble role in the natural process. It is the utterly contingent, "inconstant stay" of man, thrown against the "conceit" of the uncontingent single law of time, that justifies the use of the theatrical figure which reduces "every thing" to helpless, insubstantial puppetry.

The outside control is absolute, as the later notion of "the fools of time" makes explicit. An indifferent, pagan nature that is pure process and thus absolute in its transience controls completely. It is the nature of the influencing stars and the maddeningly "selfsame sky" that equally *ch*eer and *ch*eck (and how effective the alliteration that proves the identity, from the perspective of nature's indifference, of blessing and curse). Further, they indifferently cheer and check men and plants, or rather, more extremely, "men *as* plants." In the face of this nature, what hope can there be for man to command his "brave state" but most inconstantly? Nor can we be much impressed by the poet's chances to win his "war with Time" by destroying contingency through the human device of art.

Instead it can be only an acknowledgement and an acceptance of nature's indifference, of its treatment of "men as plants," that can convert indifference to universal blessing. By submitting to the natural order and to man's plant-like role in it, the friend can also find the resurrection granted the plant and all of nature. The amoral, indifferent egalitarianism that we as self-loving individuals attribute to a nature *out*side us we could convert to the universal blessedness provided by its immanent laws of regeneration, were we to find nature *in*side us in our reduction to communal, other-loving entities. Again the call to the pastoral, to Schiller's "naive poet." So the friend's victory over time can be won only through the common salvation urged in Sonnet 16 that, by the end of Sonnet 17, will allow the friend to be most uncommon.

For in Sonnet 16 the poet disdains the hopeful redemption by poetry promised in Sonnet 15; he foregoes the devices of man for the sole device of nature. The impotence of his verse is indicated by the phrase "barren rhyme," which surely condemns the suggested alternative to procreation, and in language appropriate to the procreative view of life. The verse, as "barren," accordingly—for all its efforts—has become the friend's "tomb" by the start of Sonnet 17. May we not carry along the crucial relation between "tomb" and "womb" from Sonnet 3?[9] Clearly, what is needed is the fertile rather than the "barren," the womb rather than the tomb. We are returned to the mirror-image, to yet another manipulation of it. We have seen it formed in the "glass of crystal clean" of Narcissus, in the eye of the beloved, in the child, in the procession of nature that is to reflect human history. Now we see it in the imitation that is art, that is, in the "painted counterfeit" (line 8). Shakespeare allows to verse the imitative characteristics of painting, perhaps in the tradition of *ut pictura poesis,* that perversion of the Aristotelian notion of imitation. Art is barren, then; the friend's children, his "living flowers," would be "liker" than his "painted counterfeit." They would be more like him in that they would be alive and substantial—incarnations—not lifeless and insubstantial. So despite any superficial resemblance, the "counterfeit" is just that and can never enact the historical role of the person and his living flowers. The counterfeit, then, suffers from the same limitations as the unmagical vanity mirror of Narcissus. It is bloodless, shuts life up, freezes it, instead of making it possible. Indeed it is tomb, as are the eyes of self-love, and not womb.

It is the use of painting that allows the effective "lines of life" (line 9) and "drawn by your own sweet skill" (line 14).[10] In language reminiscent of Sonnet 3, lines 2 and 3,

[9] The explicit relation between "tomb" and "womb" appears again in the internal rhyme between them in Sonnet 86, line 4 ("Making their tomb the womb wherein they grew"). Here, outside the procreative mood, the poet presents a more optimistic view which allows poetry to transform the tomb into womb.

[10] Of course, Shakespeare manages to have it both ways since "lines," besides being used in the painting metaphor, still vaguely carries its sense as a part of the poem. It is the word that allows him to treat one art in terms of another (lines of poetry in terms of lines of painting) while keeping it itself.

where we saw the crucial word "repair" also occur, the poet urges the inadequacy of the lines of art to keep the friend's image in repair; only the "lines of life" can do it, because only in this way can the friend give life and thus keep himself living ("To give away yourself keeps yourself still"), using a "sweet skill" beyond that of an art which freezes life. In this context "lines" refers not only to the disfiguring lines of aging (the lines of "time's pencil"[11]) and to the lines of the poet-painter (here the sublime poet-painter that is nature whose lines of life are superior to the lines of the poet's "pupil pen"), but most importantly to the most literal lines of life, the lines of living inheritance, family lines—the *line*age of communal history. Thus the only lines that can give life ("you must live," line 14) are those "drawn" by the "sweet skill" of husbandry. But to draw this way is also to draw oneself forward into history. So one lives in that the lines of life are "drawn" by his "sweet skill," and one lives in that he (his historical line) is "drawn" (that is, pulled forward) by that "sweet skill." The seeming redundancy indicates how firmly the two meanings of "drawn" have been made one. They both make singly clear that the lines drawn by man's art, instead of by man's nature, cannot preserve the life which that art imitates, but can only entomb it.

But the dialectic must run its course: the extreme antithesis of Sonnet 16 (the denial of the immortalizing power of art which was asserted in Sonnet 15) is modified in Sonnet 17, although the primacy of "breed" is maintained. Even if the poet were able totally to capture the "life" of his friend—and the limited nature of his art prevents it—his work would not be believed by the future ages, but because of the unearthly praise which would be its truth would be dismissed as mere hyperbole. Here with a fine touch of realism, uncom-

---

[11] See also Sonnet 19, lines 9–10: "O, carve not with thy hours my love's fair brow, / Nor draw no lines there with thine antique pen!"

mon in the Petrarchan convention that treated poetry as an immortalizing agent itself eternal, Shakespeare's tough common sense insists on recognizing that poems, like men, can age. They too come within the processes of time. Only a human creation after all, they too are part of the "every thing" that is subject to the scythe. Unlike the usual, unearned Petrarchan assumption of the eternal and eternalizing nature of verse (which of course Shakespeare himself freely uses elsewhere—indeed, beginning with the very sonnets which follow this one[12]), this view allows immortality only via nature, with man's poetry aging into "an antique song," reduced to "papers (yellowed with their age) / . . . scorn'd, like old men of less truth than tongue." As narcissistic man, reduced to his image in the glass, is finally reduced to the physical self that time destroys and makes food for worms, so the poetry that seeks to immortalize the narcissistic friend is reduced to its physical embodiment, the papers that, as they shrivel, seem to earn the other attributes of age as well.

The eternal youth of the poems can be ensured only by the process that ensures the ever-recurrent youth of the friend, because the credibility, and hence the life, of the

---

[12] Perhaps Shakespeare is simply being inconsistent as he moves from sonnet to sonnet, allowing each its own operational system. But I think not, at least in this case, especially in view of the language of Sonnets 18 and 19, which have such clear relations to those which precede, as the poet struggles to improve his poetry's powers to praise and to preserve. But is this necessarily inconsistent? Since Shakespeare finally acknowledges in Sonnet 17 that, if his friend will only cooperate by breeding, his praises in verse may after all have some contributory immortalizing effect, it may be that he feels he has here earned his right to follow the poem by attempts to immortalize him in verse. That is, by the end of Sonnet 17 he has set down the condition upon which the poems that follow depend if they are to do their work. It is up to his friend to play his primary role by breeding, so that, from here on, having laid down the condition and having made his final plea, the poet can only do the secondary immortalizing that is left to him in hopes that the primary has prepared the way.

poems depend on the continued existence of the friend to whom they can be compared. If the friend is "refigured" so that his form exists still, then art too can live, since it has nature's life to extend its own. The immortality in the flesh will guarantee the immortality in the word, will allow the word itself to take on flesh. ("You should live twice—in it [the child], and in my rhyme.")

This is a synthesis beyond the tentative call to art in Sonnet 15 and the outright rejection of it, in the name of nature, in Sonnet 16. For it to occur, the friend will have disdained the role of Narcissus to play the natural role of husband, and in resurrecting his image by bending linear time into circular, he is also resurrecting the poem and its efficacy. For the image given back by a reflective art is, after all, like that seen in the other mirror. If it is merely the insubstantial reflection of its subject, it turns back upon him and has life only with him, bound with him by the unyielding unmagical linearity of time. To live it must be given substance, suffering the conversion from mirror to window that can convert time to the circular; thus art becomes dependent on the very rejuvenating processes of nature in its eternal recurrence that give life to man. In a profound sense art must imitate nature only as man must, by being subordinated to nature as a part of it, as man is. For what is mirrored is nature as process, nature as an open and opening history, which is more than mirror as the circle that is somehow progressive is more than line.

The openness of the natural way has been proclaimed from the idyllic first quatrain of Sonnet 1, which precedes the unhappy alternative chosen by the narcissistic friend who is introduced with the "But" of line 5. It is the openness man is called upon to imitate—to make a reflection of himself—in a surrender of self to community and history in order to extend himself. Once more we see the biblical notion of losing oneself to find oneself, or, as we have seen Shakespeare put it in Sonnet 16, "To give away yourself keeps yourself still."[13] But, if I may turn back to Sonnet 1 and to this quatrain, the natural idyll is shown to be human idyll here too: the universal and traditional "beauty's rose" is symbol enough to support the dual burden. Then the notion of ripeness, death, and the resurrection in the "heir" which is proved by the stroke of the internal rhyme (*"bear* his memory") that acts as a phonetic demonstration of the mirror created by successive generations. After the assault on the friend as Narcissus in the second quatrain, we return to the idyll at the start of the third. The recalcitrant friend, standing at the head of the parade of nature and its energies ("the world's fresh ornament / And only herald to the gaudy spring") rejects his role, ignoring the implications of the "gaudy" in spring. And unnaturally, but still in the terms of vegetative life, "within [his] own bud buriest [his] content." Thus we shift back to the closed, the niggardly, the unnatural, in total opposition to the liberality of nature as "frank," as bestower of the "bounteous largess" (Sonnet 4).

In Sonnet 4 the harsh, unnatural discordant note is introduced, here with the crude language of the pocketbook. It is the friend as tight-fisted hoarder-usurer who subverts the generous gifts of open nature, and thus dooms them. His very niggardliness forces him to be an "unthrift," to waste himself. Here Shakespeare introduces the complicated relations among forms of "use," leading us finally to the climactic

---

[13] See also the expanded version of this notion in the octave of Sonnet 13:

> O, that you were yourself! but, love, you are
> No longer yours than you yourself here live.
> Against this coming end you should prepare
> And your sweet semblance to some other give.
> So should that beauty which you hold in lease
> Find no determination; then you were
> Yourself again after yourself's decease
> When your sweet issue your sweet form should bear.

line 11 of Sonnet 9: "And kept unus'd, the user so destroys it." He forces us into etymological awareness, reminding us of the involvement of "use" in "unused," "abuse," and especially in "usurer," who uses a signal form of abuse or misuse.[14] This specially cursed form of usury is "profitless," thus even being deprived of the one advantage for which the detestable practice is undertaken. The oxymoron, "profitless usurer," developed from "abuse" (line 5), introduces the play on relations among use, death, and life. The friend is charged with "abuse" because he has stopped the chain of giving; because, having been given, he himself keeps instead of giving in his turn. He will not imitate the "frankness" of nature with his own, refusing to mirror nature, rejecting nature's open uses for the closed use of the inbred self. If this strange use be usury, it is profitless since he cannot keep long but can only destroy. So line 7 concludes with "use," ironically the rhyme for "abuse." Surely this "use" is still "abuse," as the rhyme helps indicate: it is improper use that, depriving others, finally deprives self; that, in refusing to spend, exhausts totally. It is a use that refuses to use, only to end by using up. This improper use, in using up, stands opposed to life (". . . why dost thou use / So great a sum of sums, yet canst not live"). This use that is the negation of use, by refusing marriage, literally prevents life; it leads to the "unus'd beauty" that "must be tomb'd" (and must not the relation of "tomb" to "womb" in the previous sonnet be carried over?). In the final line, the alternative use, proper use, is tied to life through the life it creates. And the lineage of the giving of gifts, the movement from legacy to legacy that ensures a history that is both repetition and progression, is

[14] We may be reminded also of Donne's use of the same essential strategy with "sense" and "absence" in *A Valediction Forbidding Mourning* (see above, p. 15). In both cases phonetic coincidence is transformed into an identity that has substantive justification in the poem's construction of its peculiar philology.

extended. The words which concluded lines 7 and 8 in such critical opposition ("use," "live") are here in the last line happily joined in mutual dependence ("Which, *used, lives* th' executor to be"). For the earlier "use" was the negation of use as the earlier "live," because of that earlier "use," was the negation of life ("canst *not* live").

The total sense of the key line 12 of Sonnet 9 is now perfectly obvious:

> Is it for fear to wet a widow's eye
> That thou consum'st thyself in single life?
> Ah! if thou issueless shalt hap to die,
> The world will wail thee like a makeless wife;
> The world will be thy widow, and still weep
> That thou no form of thee hast left behind
> When every private widow well may keep,
> By children's eyes, her husband's shape in mind.
> Look, what an unthrift in the world doth spend
> Shifts but his place, for still the world enjoys it;
> But beauty's waste hath in the world an end,
> And kept unus'd, the user so destroys it.
>   No love toward others in that bosom sits
>   That on himself such murd'rous shame commits.

The full power of "waste" (line 11), that which is used up, echoes the forceful verb ("consum'st") in line 2 that reaches out in several directions and to several sonnets. An equivalence that permits substitutions among the terms has been established among "unus'd," "user," and "destroys" in that line 12: this unuse, far from preserving, uses, indeed uses up, and so destroys. Thus the use that is unuse justifies the charge of wrongdoing beyond that of the normal (and lesser) "unthrift," who hurts himself but not "the world"[15] and demon-

---

[15] The words "the world" are used in three successive lines (9–11) after occurring at the opening of both lines 4 and 5 above, thus indicating the certainty of emphasis (or over-emphasis) with which the poet confers the communal and historical obligation on his friend.

strates the mutual dependence of self-hatred and social hatred instead of their mutual opposition ("No love toward others in that bosom sits / That on himself such murd'rous shame commits"). And it is their mutual opposition upon which self-love is mistakenly predicated. So miserliness beyond all misers, reckless spending beyond all spendthrifts, the vain, self-loving, acquisitive grasping of the world's rights beyond all usurers, and the self-destructive drive of the suicide—all these paradoxically at once through an improper use that is both a negation of use and a using up. They spring from a refusal to use any but the unmagical, prosaic mirror, a refusal to forego it for the mirror that is more than mirror, that allows use to multiply itself through the miracle of incarnation.

As there is another and better "use"—use to preserve—so there is another and better "usury," usury that offers its increment to the world ("That use is not forbidden usury," Sonnet 6, line 5). In Sonnet 6 the cold calculations of the practical arithmetic of the business world have been enlisted on the side of the pulsing, magical cause of the gods. But we cannot pursue the strange logic of the poem without first retreating to the previous sonnet. For in Sonnets 5 and 6 we come across the first of many cases in this sequence (we have already examined Sonnets 15–17 as a unit) in which, poetically and rhetorically, we are dealing with a single twenty-eight line unit, one whose structure cries out against the impropriety of stopping after line 14 or of beginning afresh with line 15. Let us, then, look at Sonnets 5 and 6 in order:

> Those hours that with gentle work did frame
> The lovely gaze where every eye doth dwell,
> Will play the tyrants to the very same
> And that unfair which fairly doth excel;
> For never-resting time leads summer on

To hideous winter and confounds him there,
Sap check'd with frost and lusty leaves quite gone,
Beauty o'ersnow'd and bareness everywhere.
Then, were not summer's distillation left
A liquid prisoner pent in walls of glass,
Beauty's effect with beauty were bereft—
Nor it, nor no remembrance what it was;
But flowers distill'd, though they with winter meet,
Leese but their show—their substance still lives sweet.

Then let not winter's ragged hand deface
In thee thy summer ere thou be distill'd.
Make sweet some vial; treasure thou some place
With beauty's treasure ere it be self-kill'd.
That use is not forbidden usury
Which happies those that pay the willing loan:
That's for thyself to breed another thee,
Or ten times happier, be it ten for one.
Ten times thyself were happier than thou art,
If ten of thine ten times refigur'd thee.
Then what could death do if thou shouldst depart
Leaving thee living in posterity?
Be not self-will'd, for thou art much too fair
To be death's conquest and make worms thine heir.

Sonnet 5, being only the first half, concentrates on the
happy solution nature has found to the problem of age and
death. It is but the pastoral framework, with the specific injunction to the friend to play his proper pastoral role de-
ferred until the second half. The brilliance of Sonnet 5 derives
largely from the applicability of the language of nature to the
human world, the proving of union or even identity through
metaphor such as we have witnessed before. It opens with a
general statement concerning the effect of time on the friend,
paragon of all beauty, the imminent total destruction of his
beauty being proved in language by the coinage that makes

"unfair" a transitive verb which negates, totally cancels, the "fairly." In the fashion of pastoral we turn at once to time in nature and the march of the seasons. But this is no mere transfer from tenor to vehicle, for we never really leave the human at all. The life of nature is here not merely a reflection of the life of man; it is *both* reflection—a mirror—and substantively the thing itself: it *is* the life of man.[16] What begins as analogy becomes identity. And once again the language proves it.

I refer not to anything so slight as "hideous" or "confounds," but to the far more inescapable figure of the "sap" as Shakespeare handles it. Line 7 is a highly dramatic line and properly introduces the poet's major movement to work his magic and justify his claim. The rhythmic pattern corroborates its key position. After the relentless surge of metrical regularity that carries us through line 5 and the terminal quality of line 6, there is the absolute stoppage in the twin accents that open line 7, a stoppage that echoes the frozen immobility of "Sap check'd with frost. . . ." The rest of the line forces us to extend "sap" beyond its most literal limitations, thanks to the alliterative "lusty leaves" which phonetically yoke natural and human meanings, the "lusty" also casting its shadow backward to the "sap." Further, the "frost," which acts on the sap, is juxtaposed to "lusty" and is another agent that brings "sap" and "lusty" to a single, double-visioned area of meaning. But the frost that o'ersnows beauty does not conquer totally after all: "summer's distillation" remains in liquid form, with the "walls of glass" both its prison and its sanctuary that preserves the living substance for the successive generation of the following spring. Of course, most obviously "walls of glass" here mean the walls of ice that protect the sap even as they "check" it. Both the liquid state and the prisoner state of the "liquid prisoner" are

---

[16] Or so it ought to be, unless man rejects the role indicated by this substantive equation, as his friend threatens to.

ensured by the ice, that which, as we have seen in the earlier "frost," is the enemy to liquid, is its frozen state, its state of unuse. The miracle of sap, of "distillation," converts this destructive agent into the guarantor of future creativity. The human, sexual equivalent of procreation can hardly be missed: there is the full significance of sap, there is implied the womb within the "walls of glass" confirmed by the "vial" that the friend is urged to "make sweet" (Sonnet 6, line 3), and above all there is the complex process of distillation which reaches out in several directions, all of them close to man and his reproduction. First, the distillation, which has retreated from its showplace to its haven within the walls of glass, is a rarefied reduction to essence, the pure form of the flower which awaits its next incarnation. Secondly, the distillation is, quite literally, a dripping down, suggesting of course the act of fertilizing, the making "sweet some vial." Finally, distillation is in a way a dissolving—indeed in several ways. On the level of natural imagery, as *summer's* distillation it is a dissolved form of ice; and in thus becoming a solution of the threat of ice to immobilize, it becomes the life-saving liquid on the human level into which the other level naturally flows. It is life in the midst of death: as the seminal fluid that guarantees the ever-returning April, it is the dissolution of the ice that is death. The paradox of the fluid at once contained and preserved by the antagonistic and destructive agent would seem to be a new version of the conventional Petrarchan paradox that made so much of the strange state of ice. And of course primarily—and explicitly—the liquid is "prisoner" of the "walls of glass," as if the ice, true to its service of the immobile, were *actively* containing it, keeping it from flowing abroad to bring the world to new birth. The fluid is locked in, unable to transform the ice even as the ice cannot reduce it to its own state. How much more effective the Petrarchan paradox has become with its two sides now but two forms of a single element. But, unlike the unyielding ice-fire paradox of the Petrarchan convention, this one ends one-sidedly, the ice becoming liquid even if this special liquid never becomes ice. At last the soluble ice will dissolve, and life will out, for the indestructible sap was only "check'd with frost" but never solidified by it.

Can we see beyond the paradoxical relations between ice and liquid to the one between mirror and window, also two ways with one element? The word "glass" in the "walls of glass" may allow us to do it, if we may borrow from the immediate context of the surrounding sonnets in order to make "glass" perform a double service, meaning mirror as well as ice. Surely we may properly wonder why Shakespeare chose to use the term "glass" here and thus constructed a secondary metaphor for his metaphor of ice. As we do, even though there is no pressure in this sonnet for glass as mirror, we cannot help but have the sense of mirror intrude upon the word at least secondarily, especially as we discover the mirror-symbolism we have been looking into elsewhere to be but an extension of the original metaphor of ice. This becomes another evidence of the unifying control with which this sonnet moves up and down the broad range of natural and human possibilities, bringing them all to life at a touch, the brilliant and plastic touch of language. The effect of ice—of the walls of glass—is to check the sap, to imprison the life-giving liquid, to shut it up with itself, preventing its outward flow which can revitalize the dying world outside. But is not this precisely what the unmagical mirror, the "glass of crystal clean," was seen to do in its shutting up life with itself? By keeping it locked within its own eyes, Narcissus-like, the mirror—another and yet the same wall of glass—could freeze all life by stopping its historical flow. It is trapped in a self-enclosed world of mirrors, walls of glass from which there is no escape but the escape from self. So in moving to nature and the retransforming of ice into its liquid state, we have not left humanity and the retransforming of the mirror that congeals life into the window that looses it. The sequel in Sonnet 6 confirms these equations by returning us, by way of distillation, to humanity and the mirror. The poet asks his friend to be "distill'd" before winter manages to "deface" his summer. By "deface," the key word, we must understand more than just *destroy*, its generalized meaning. We must take it literally: it is the removal of his face that is feared. And this is the fear of the end that narcissism forces upon itself: the self-love enclosed in the "glass of crystal clean" that has the face removed with the life. It is why the poet has pleaded for the regeneration that would have the face come again and again, that would get the friend outward, through the looking-glass, into history. The ice and glass must be gone *through* together. An important echo of "deface," and the alternative to it, occurs in line 10 with the word "refigur'd." Once more it is the secondary meaning that does it, though, given its context, this meaning insists on asserting itself. For beyond the obvious, light, arithmetical play, it is the reappearance, the multiplication, of the very *figure* of the friend—his form and features—that the poet prays for as the "usury" that is "not forbidden," indeed is even blessed.[17] Otherwise the poet must face that other usury, stemming from the use that is abuse, a using up, through unuse. This wrongful use stems from the friend's being "self-will'd" (line 13), an echo in sound and meaning of its consequence, the "beauty's treasure" that is "self-kill'd" (line 4). All that is left is death—and the worms: "To be death's

[17] This literal use of "figure" in "refigur'd" is surely supported by the typological use of *"figura"* which we saw concern Auerbach so centrally in his treatment of the medieval world. In other sonnets we shall see a much more serious—and crucial—use of the "figure" in Biblical typology. As the friend is here the aboriginal archetype, a "fulfillment" at the very start in the initial "figure" that is to be repeated ("refigur'd"), so elsewhere he is more typically the "fulfillment" that stands at the end of a long history of pre-figures.

conquest and make worms thine heir." It is especially ironic to name worms as the heir of the narcissistic misuser when we recall it is the preservative role of the rightful heir (remember "tender *heir* might *bear* his memory" in Sonnet 1) that has initiated this entire group.

2. *TRUTH VS. TROTH: THE WORMS*
OF THE VILE, WISE WORLD

WORMS become an important recurrent symbol that is related to all I have been tracing here. Shakespeare has provided for them from his first sonnet. In referring earlier to the final line of Sonnet 1 ("To eat the world's due, by the grave and thee"), I saw the friend characterized "not only as a collaborator of death but as one who anticipates death by doing the worm's destructive work on this side of the tomb." The claim is justified in retrospect, from the view of later sonnets in which the worms explicitly enter as agents of obliteration. But the word "eat" has anticipated them in making the friend one of them. And so he is: for by denying the world an heir, he has reduced his reality to the dimensions of the physical self which he uses up, indeed which, as niggardly glutton, he feeds upon in the mere act of living.[1] There is nothing left for any heir but the worms; having rejected his incarnation in the beloved's heart or in a son, he can live on only in the worms. Thus the world of Narcissus—the world of self-love—becomes the world of worms, and both of them the world reduced to its dead physical level, life in its unelevated material dimension, the dimension that must deny the intangible, deny that anything can transform the unmagical mirror that closes itself up.

Self-love and the broader world of self-interest: we have seen it is but a short step for Shakespeare from the world of

---

[1] So intent is Shakespeare upon this notion of gluttony that in Sonnet 2 he uses the phrase, "All-eating shame" (line 8), even though there is nothing in the poem to justify or give precise meaning to the epithet. Of course, in the context of the surrounding sonnets, the meaning is clear enough, although the phrase remains unfortunate, especially in this sonnet, where it relates to nothing else. Here is one of many cases where treating the *Sonnets* as one body permits us to extend its cross-references to the systematic fullness of glossary.

worms to the materialistic world that calls for tangible—and profitable—results. For the two are really the same world: the world of worms, a vile world, and the shrewd world of practical wisdom—the "wise world" that is vile in much the same way. It is this equation that forces upon us the bitter irony of the deceptive Sonnets 71 and 72:

No longer mourn for me when I am dead
Than you shall hear the surly sullen bell
Give warning to the world that I am fled
From this vile world, with vilest worms to dwell.
Nay, if you read this line, remember not
The hand that writ it; for I love you so
That I in your sweet thoughts would be forgot
If thinking on me then should make you woe.
O, if, I say, you look upon this verse
When I, perhaps, compounded am with clay,
Do not so much as my poor name rehearse,
But let your love even with my life decay,
    Lest the wise world should look into your moan
    And mock you with me after I am gone.

O, lest the world should task you to recite
What merit liv'd in me, that you should love
After my death, dear love, forget me quite,
For you in me can nothing worthy prove;
Unless you would devise some virtuous lie,
To do more for me than mine own desert
And hang more praise upon deceased I
Than niggard truth would willingly impart.
O, lest your true love may seem false in this,
That you for love speak well of me untrue,
My name be buried where my body is,
And live no more to shame nor me nor you!
    For I am sham'd by that which I bring forth,
    And so should you, to love things nothing worth.

The poet in these sonnets is pleading with his beloved friend to cooperate with time and the world, and in two ways: by not allowing love to outlast the poet's life and by not bestowing more value on the poet and his work than is warranted by the cold objectivity of fact. But what is the nature of this world to which the friend is to conform? It is the "vile world" from which the poet, in dying, appears voluntarily to have "fled." And what about it is vile more than those very attributes which the friend is here solicited to share? In dying away from the "vile world," the poet will dwell with "vilest worms." The movement from the positive to the superlative degree of the same adjective, "vile" to "vilest," in moving from "world" to "worms," is crucial (especially as we feel even the nouns echoing each other): the worms are the furthest extension of the very tendency that makes the world "vile." The world as practical time-server that takes material truth as its total reality has the quality that is most purely represented in the activity of the worms. The vile world is a lesser worm: as I have said, it in effect does the worm's work on this side of the tomb. This is the aspect of the world with which the friend is called upon to join in its practical assault upon the more-than-material. His "love" is to "decay" (and this is the perfect verb) even as the poet's "life" does; he is to feed on the body of love as the worms do on the body of life, since he is to see both bodies as suffering the identical limitation of the flesh. The poem itself, as always in Petrarchism, defies time by outliving the body, but the friend must not let this transcendence deter his coldblooded allegiance to the world. For his attempt to echo this transcendence of time can win him only "woe" and the mockery of "the wise world," the world whose wiseness is synonymous with its vileness. The shift from the "vile world" (line 4) to the "wise world" (line 13) is the final evidence of Shakespeare's irony. For this world is wise—that is, shrewd, prudential—only as it is vile, only as it exercises those characteristics which ape the destructive perfection, the absolute cooperation with time, of the "vilest worms." How single-mindedly, then, is his friend to take this selfless, seemingly anti-sentimental injunction to obey the dictates of the world's cold wisdom lest he be mocked by it?

Sonnet 72 leads from the impracticality of mourning to the untruth of love's eulogy. Again the pressure upon the friend comes from the world both wise and vile ("lest the world should task you"), so that the poet finally must be as distrustful of the virtue of truth as he was of the virtue of avoiding woe. The friend can justify his mourning to the world only by citing the poet's great "merit," a merit the poet denies exists in fact. According to this world, only that emotion is to be spent which is adequately repaid by the value, the "worth" of its object. Hence the monetary sense of "things nothing worth" in the last line (a transformation of the more general "nothing worthy" in line 4) and of the adjective "niggard" as it is applied to "truth." The truth of the world is a niggard, miserly in the precision and ungenerosity of its measurement of claim against fact and thus in its imputation of the lie. The lie would make the friend "seem false," although this very falseness would be evidence of his "true love." The apparent paradox is heightened by the tightness of repetition in the language of lines 9–10: the poet infers that the "true love" is proved in that "you for love speak well of me untrue." A love is true to the extent that it forces speech that is untrue. Clearly the judgment of what is untrue is rendered by the "niggard truth" that rules the vile, wise world. This is the world that dictates—in the name of that truth and its practicality—that the poet's "name be buried where [his] body is," that it be reduced to his fleshly limitations and dwell "with vilest worms" as their victim, as it is the victim of time and the world, which they symbolize.

Of course what makes finally bitter the poet's plea that the friend join the world and measure his worth by unexaggerated fact alone is our knowledge that, as Petrarchan sonneteer, the poet has been fully indulging the convention of praising his friend in the most lavish terms he could find and of explicitly trying to immortalize his name and virtues by the magic of a poetry that would long outlast frail flesh. His sonnets have been both act and repository of faith. The poet, then, has— from the standpoint of the world's truth—been a Petrarchan liar and a foolish resister of the unconquerable worms. In return he asks of the friend a less valiant and less outmoded gesture: that the poet be viewed with the cold killing eye of fact and not the incarnating eye of love. His bitterness here seems addressed not to the friend but to the world that would exact such a loss of faith, such a niggardly narrowing of truth.

The assertion that the love is true in its untruth—indeed through its untruth—is evidence of another sort of truth that is unniggardly, that is all generosity, that makes groundless exaggeration the test of that truth. This, of course, is truth as fidelity, an antique, chivalric virtue that surpasses the understanding of the wise and vile world of niggardly efficiency, the world of worms. There is a revolt here against the very epistemology of the materialistic world, against the criterion for truth in a faithless world, a revolt in the name of an older and less stringent epistemology. We might for convenience term it the conflict between truth and troth, really meaning by them two kinds of truth, one measured by unyielding objective fact and the other by the heart of love. In this conflict, we may properly see the two kinds of mirror we have found earlier. For the niggardly truth of the wise world is controlled by the naive epistemology of a mirror-reality, with the eye as the "glass of crystal clean" that reflects all that is. Here is the worldly man's phenomenalism in his addiction to the tangible world of appearance; here is the extension of what we have seen to be the closed, tomb-like world of Narcissus to the wise world of the worms and its entombing doctrine. Rejected is the troth that reflects and creates more

than is there, that makes miraculous claims out of a fidelity
that dares *"seem* false" to observable fact.

The strange, unworldly logic of love can also make its
claims, although for Shakespeare they must ironically take
the tangible shape of their materialistic antagonist. Sonnet 74
is cast totally in the matter-of-factness of apparently common-
sense logic, a tone especially marked in its contrast to the rich
and melancholy imagery of Sonnet 73, the first half of the
two-sonnet sequence in which the poet speaks of his approaching death and the friend's approaching loss.[2]

> But be contented. When that fell arrest
> Without all bail shall carry me away,
> My life hath in this line some interest,
> Which for memorial still with thee shall stay.
> When thou reviewest this, thou dost review
> The very part was consecrate to thee.
> The earth can have but earth, which is his due;
> My spirit is thine, the better part of me.
> So then thou hast but lost the dregs of life,
> The prey of worms, my body being dead—
> The coward conquest of a wretch's knife,
> Too base of thee to be remembered.
>   The worth of that is that which it contains,
>   And that is this, and this with thee remains.

And yet the sensible business-like tone is the basis for a most
unmaterialistic claim. The conversational opening, with its
full stop, indicates not only the rhetorical dependence of the
sonnet upon Sonnet 73 but also its strong contrast to it in tone
and in the firm consolation for the sadness of loss. The mono-
syllabic precision, seen most clearly in lines 7 and 9 and the
couplet but apparent throughout, establishes the seeming
hard-headed reasonability of the poet's insistence, as does his

---

[2] All but the couplet of Sonnet 73 is quoted on pp. 98–99 above.

use of the language of the marketplace. He is, in his "fell arrest," to be carried away without "bail," though the "interest" left by his life will remain with his friend since the "earth," in collecting his body (*his* "earth," as also in Sonnet 146, line 1), will have its own, which is all the payment "due" it.

The poet's confidence is made possible by the fact that his poem, this sonnet, is a tangible entity—a material thing that endures—even as it is the container of his spirit. He offers it, itself a miraculous mirror-window, in evidence of the mirror-window miracle of love. The "interest," the "memorial," beyond the "due" claims of "earth," is the "this" of line 5 which has at once its existence (as thing) and its more-than-material power (as container of spirit—line 8 and the couplet) proved by the mere fact of the friend's reading it. In the poem the spirit is made flesh with the word. Shakespeare forces the point by making it true of the most commonplace word, even the mere pointing and grunting that create demonstrative pronouns. Thus the brilliantly cryptic precision of the couplet, with the intensity and the simplicity of its discovery:

> The worth of that is that which it contains,
> And that is this, and this with thee remains.

Only the demonstratives, set in motion earlier by line 5, could totally make his case in accordance with the marketplace rules he must here abide by. By contrast, the filled-out paraphrase would seem like a high and untried claim: the value of my spirit is equal to the value of what holds it, and what holds it is this poem which still is yours after my death. The vile, wise world could easily snicker, while as the couplet now reads it makes the entire poem a successful attack on that world using that world's own weapons. Nor does he neglect its symbol, the worms. This world is bound by the "earth" and can claim only this much of the poet. But here the poet is more openly defiant of the earthly claim than he was in the more guarded Sonnets

71–72 (see Sonnet 71, especially lines 4, 10, 12; and Sonnet 72, especially line 11). What is lost to "earth" (by being buried within it and thus also returned to it) is his "earth," "the dregs of life," and—most important—"the prey of worms," which are the agents of "earth," doing its work, exacting its claim. Worthy only of earth, his "body being dead" is now (in contrast to 71–72) too base to be remembered, though it leaves the worthiness of his spirit (and poems) unaffected. For also allied with the wise destructive world of earth and worms is the "wretch's knife" with its "coward conquest" of bodies. Surely we are to see in the "wretch's knife" an ignoble reduction of time with his sickle, the grim reaper who frequently appears in the sonnets (see especially Sonnets 60, 63, 116, 123, 124, 126). Here he is transformed to a lowly assassin, fit brother to the worms and fellow-agent of the shrewd world that delegates full control to them. The incarnating power of love again breaks through the death-driven, self-enclosed mirror (earth to earth) of the wise, feeding world and furnishes proof of the irony behind the cynical disclaimers of Sonnets 71–72.

The most profound identification of the feeding world with the body, death, and worms occurs in Sonnet 146:

> Poor soul, the centre of my sinful earth,
> ... these rebel pow'rs that thee array,
> Why dost thou pine within and suffer dearth,
> Painting thy outward walls so costly gay?
> Why so large cost, having so short a lease,
> Dost thou upon thy fading mansion spend?
> Shall worms, inheritors of this excess,
> Eat up thy charge? Is this thy body's end?
> Then, soul, live thou upon thy servant's loss,
> And let that pine to aggravate thy store;
> Buy terms divine in selling hours of dross;
> Within be fed, without be rich no more.

So shalt thou feed on Death, that feeds on men,
And Death once dead, there's no more dying then.

The alternatives are clear in what seems to be an obvious enough Platonism: either the soul feeds on the body or the body feeds on the soul. In the latter case, all is reduced to the flesh and dies with it. In the former case, all is reduced to soul through an asceticism that anticipates and thus defeats death by voluntarily making the body its victim and depriving death and his worms of what was to have been theirs. But by now Shakespeare can easily tighten and enlarge this claim through the identifications his metaphors have achieved.

In the early lines the poet struggles to achieve a manageable and even graphic figure of the relation between soul and body as the relation between reality and appearance, between unchanging core and a moving periphery. He briefly suggests an astronomical and a political image as well as the more obvious notion of the body as the "fading mansion" that houses the soul.[3] The use of "earth" in the opening line is most helpful in conjunction with "centre." As the earth is center of the universe, so the soul is center of the earth, of *his* earth—the sinful, fading, feeding flesh destined for the feeding worms. Thus the very cosmic order gives centricity to the soul, makes it the proper governing power. But the body,

---

[3] I believe the mansion image is not altogether helpful in its relation to the vehicles of the other images in the sonnet. Ideally the image that moves us from the rebellious servant to the feeding worms should deal with a form of life; for, although we can make the activity of the worms applicable to the mansion, this image does not seem to me an appropriate extension of the worm-ridden world of flesh we have, with Shakespeare, been examining. Of course, if we think only of the prose meaning, the mansion—with its costly walls and neglected interior, its large cost and short lease, and its being inherited—fits the materialistic consideration that colors Shakespeare's metaphors in many of the sonnets, even if it leads us to violate the proper extension of the image by seeing the worms eat up the "excess" of the body rather than of the overdone "outward walls."

properly the mere ornamental "servant" of the soul to perform fleetingly in the world of appearance, has become a
"rebel." There has been an inversion of governor-subject
relations as the body has become the "end" instead of the
superficial means to the higher end which the cosmos has
ordained.

It is in accordance with this perversion of its proper "end"
that Shakespeare puns so effectively in asking later in line 8,
"Is this thy body's end?" We are to answer both yes and no.
Yes, it is, alas, the inevitable "end"—that is, terminus—of
the fleshly career to be food for the worms. But read this way,
the question is asked angrily: is this all that the presumptuous
rebel can come to? Then how dare it presume upon the
rightful order? How dare it not accept its proper role as
"servant," as mere "charge" of the soul? And this is to demand, how dare the body not accept its ordained "end"—that
is, purpose, final cause—of serving the soul as a true subject?
But this reading is to make us shout "no"—it is not the body's
end as "charge" of the soul to be inherited by worms, to feed
them. It has a higher end. Line 9 can continue with an
italicized "thou"; *you*, soul, feed in your way upon the body
during its life, reducing the "excess" which a self-pampering
body would accumulate, though only in the end for your
rivals, the worms. But the rivalry between soul and worms
over the body is of course a rivalry between ways of life, or
rather between the way of life and the way of death. It is the
rivalry between the miraculous and finally victorious way and
the vile, wise, materialistic, and finally destructive way. Hence
the appropriateness of the terms of legacy, of cost and of
reality, but above all of the language of gluttony. For it is
once more the self-interested body that, in feeding itself, is
allowing the future feeding of the worms; that prepares itself
as the worms' banquet while it sacrifices all to preparing its
own.

If the body is starved to feed the soul in its way of feeding, then death is starved with the worms. There is nothing to die as all will live in the soul—or rather nothing will die but the starved death itself. Thus "Death" in the couplet draws together within itself the multiple identities Shakespeare has earned in the sonnet: sin, earth, body, and the metonymic worms. In feeding on one, the soul feeds on them all. Even this late in the sequence we have not left the metaphorical structure of Sonnet 1 (especially as corroborated by the last line of Sonnet 6), but have extended and deepened it. Self-love is still equated with the worship of the physical and with the worship of death through the use of gluttony as the sole worldly vice (". . . or else this glutton be, / To eat the world's due, by the grave and thee") and the use of worms as the body's sole heir (". . . for thou art much too fair / To be death's conquest and make worms thine heir").

If we try to take the present doubtful ordering of the sonnets so seriously as to justify the placement of Sonnet 146,[4] we should not be surprised to find it surrounded by the accusing and self-accusing sonnets to the "black beauty" which curse the dark hellishness she both represents and inspires. We may see Sonnet 146 as reflecting the poet's condemnation of the physical love—mere fleshly appetite—for the woman and his adulation of his spiritualized Platonic love for the man (an opposition much like that in Sonnet 144). Physical desire is now representative of the deadly destructive as narcissism was in the opening sonnet. Indeed they are at root identical rather than opposed for Shakespeare, since he here sees sexual love—in an almost Sartrean view—as but an extension of self-love in its urge to self-gratification. In opposition to it is the love that can open outward toward another,

---

[4] And nowhere in this essay would I argue in favor of or against any ordering of them, beyond assuming the likelihood that here and there certain sonnets are neighboring to one another. Indeed, my attempt to make a metaphorical system of them rather requires that I view them as if they were a single entity, written simultaneously.

that can defy the limits of the material world through its
Platonic miracle. Yet by attributing the action of feeding to it
as well (Sonnet 146, lines 12 and 13), he has it use the
categories of the world it transcends. Only the immaterial
soul can feed itself without destroying itself, for by feeding on
the body it magically opens itself to otherness. It breaks
through the self-enclosure of self-aggrandizement which characterizes the lusty lover of the late sonnets as it characterizes
the Narcissus of the earliest. The unmagical mirror of self-
interest breeds the worms of vile wisdom in the one case as
in the other, if we look with the soul's eye of troth instead of
with the body's eyes that are mirror of the world's truth.

In Sonnet 113 we find this troth the poet's central concern
as he makes a most ambitious claim, even if he undercuts it
with the more sober sequel in Sonnet 114.

> Since I left you, mine eye is in my mind;
> And that which governs me to go about
> Doth part his function and is partly blind,
> Seems seeing, but effectually is out;
> For it no form delivers to the heart
> Of bird, of flow'r, or shape which it doth latch;
> Of his quick objects hath the mind no part,
> Nor his own vision holds what it doth catch;
> For if it see the rud'st or gentlest sight,
> The most sweet favour or deformed'st creature,
> The mountain or the sea, the day or night,
> The crow or dove, it shapes them to your feature.
>   Incapable of more, replete with you,
>   My most true mind thus mak'th mine eye untrue.

The final line clearly places us within the epistemological conflict of Sonnet 72 ("O, lest your true love may seem false in
this, / That you for love speak well of me untrue"). In Sonnet 113, the poet's eye, supposedly the accurate mirror of the
world of appearances according to the naive epistemology of

"truth," "effectually is out." It resigns its function of serving
"truth" in order to be faithful to the higher truth of fidelity
that I have been terming "troth." For it subjects itself and its
"quick objects" to the "mind" and the kind of vision the mind
requires. And the mind requires that all phenomena be shaped
to the "feature" of the friend, that they equally share in a universally golden world. All is seen under the aspect—and
through the shaping eyes—of faith and love. It is much like the
aspect of eternity, God's, in its indifferent viewing of opposites:
"rud'st or gentlest sight," "most sweet favour or deformed'st
creature," mountain or sea, day or night, crow or dove. All is
the oneness of beauty in love as all is the oneness of good in
God; and from Plato we know of the identity of beauty and
goodness. The aspect of love is thus as godlike in its joining of
the amoral to the moral as in its joining of the opposites. It is as
much beyond all moral judgment as it is beyond all the distinctions that mark our phenomenal world. This is the complete
deification of his love. His mind is as "replete" with that love,
has spun his world as completely out of it, as God is full of
goodness and has spun His world out of that. Thus the true-
ness of his mind surely dwarfs the insignificant untruth of his
eye: after all, while the eye may be made "untrue," the mind
—agent of the lie—is nothing less than "*most* true."

But Shakespeare is too much the realist to have his miracle
cheaply and not to distrust any extension of the psychological
fact of hallucination. As skeptic he maintains his footing in
common sense by adding Sonnet 114:

> Or whether doth my mind, being crown'd with you,
> Drink up the monarch's plague, this flattery?
> Or whether shall I say mine eye saith true,
> And that your love taught it this alchemy,
> To make of monsters and things indigest
> Such cherubins as your sweet self resemble,
> Creating every bad a perfect best

As fast as objects to his beams assemble?
O, 'tis the first! 'Tis flatt'ry in my seeing,
And my great mind most kingly drinks it up.
Mine eye well knows what with his gust is greeing,
And to his palate doth prepare the cup.
    If it be poison'd, 'tis the lesser sin
    That mine eye loves it and doth first begin.

The magic of true "alchemy" or the fraud of "flattery?" Again there is in Sonnet 114 the description of the alchemy performed upon the world by the eye in its service of the mind's faith—the divine transformation of "monsters and things indigest" into "cherubins" like the friend, of "every bad" into "a perfect best."[5] Here this description is accompanied by the explicit claim that, thanks to the magic of alchemy, this troth has its own kind of truth (". . . mine eye saith true"). But this time there is opposed to it the skeptical alternative possibility that this vision of the world is but delusion, a misguided failure of mirror-truth, a lie forced upon the docile eyes by the mind in search of wish-fulfillment. And, despite the apparent

---

[5] The godlike nature of this transformation is more apparent if we view these lines of Sonnet 114 with the help of the first quatrain of Sonnet 33, which describes the effects of the "celestial face" of morning:

> Full many a glorious morning have I seen
> Flatter the mountain tops with sovereign eye,
> Kissing with golden face the meadows green,
> Gilding pale streams with heavenly alchemy . . .

Here we move from the merely courteous—if kingly—flattering of the mountains, to the contact of the golden kiss upon the meadows, to the transforming miracle of "heavenly alchemy" within the flowing streams. The similar conjunction of flattery and alchemy, and the relation of the first to the merely kingly and the courtly, deepen the effectiveness of Sonnet 114 in the light of Sonnet 33. The parallel between the two is even more evident when we add the word "beams" (Sonnet 114, line 8) which obviously forces us momentarily to see the eye as the flattering sun of Sonnet 33. We shall see much the same grouping touched upon again, if ever so slightly and delicately, in Sonnet 87, the next to be examined.

victory at the close of Sonnet 113, the poet here retreats, for it is this latter alternative he chooses as the juster description.

This alternative is rendered completely through the extended metaphor of king, court, and the drink of flattery. The poet's mind has been "crown'd" by the friend in that the love of the friend has made it sovereign over the courtier-eyes and able to impose its will upon them. But this imposition has its price: as king the mind is subject to "the monarch's plague," the drink served up by the sycophantic eyes who would give the king what he wants. And the mind, anxious as a king to believe the flatterer, "most kingly drinks . . . up" the cup that has been prepared to his taste. The cup could be "poison'd," it seems to me, only in that it renders the drinker dangerously unfit for the world and its unyielding facts since, like all flattery, it yields untruth. In the couplet, however, the poet withdraws the charge that the courtier-eyes are insincere and lessens their guilt in preparing the deadly cup by acknowledging they are themselves in love with the flattering version of reality and, convinced by their own handiwork, themselves are the first to drink the poison from the cup. Thus Shakespeare takes back much of what, in his modest retreat to homely truth, he has given away. When, at the start of the sestet, the poet chose between flattery and alchemy—"O, 'tis the first!"—his tone seemed to me to imply a sighing acceptance of the world's meager truth together with a resigned abandonment of the divine dream. But now, in the couplet, we discover that even the fawning eyes are themselves persuaded of the golden world they envision, under the aegis of the mind, through the mediation of the friend's form— the very world that the poet has given up as delusion to the world of actuality, seen through the metaphor of crude political reality.

The need to live in the wise world may force the letdown from miracle under the threat of the poisoned cup; but the alternative can never win the allegiance of faith, which must

drink away royally, cherishing to the end the troth which is
its own brand of truth, however false to that niggard, mirror-
reality. And how fitting is the extended metaphor that has
the real, cynical world of unmiraculous truth take on the
character of the fawning politic world of courtly flattery that
shrewdly deceives with its poison—the narrow Machiavellian
world that combines all of small wiseness with its vileness.
But the richness of the false miracle that stems from troth can
alone convert even the deceiving courtly flatterer, the eyes—
in contradiction to all they know as mirroring agents—into
true believers in what they must know as false, into faithful
victims of their own poison.

Perhaps our definitive word on the promises and deceptions
of truth should be spoken by Sonnet 87, which turns out to
be a non-Petrarchan commentary on the Petrarchan lover's
lowliness.

> Farewell! thou art too dear for my possessing,
> And like enough thou know'st thy estimate.
> The charter of thy worth gives thee releasing;
> My bonds in thee are all determinate.
> For how do I hold thee but by thy granting,
> And for that riches where is my deserving?
> The cause of this fair gift in me is wanting,
> And so my patent back again is swerving.
> Thyself thou gav'st, thy own worth then not knowing,
> Or me, to whom thou gav'st it, else mistaking:
> So thy great gift, upon misprision growing,
> Comes home again, on better judgment making.
>   Thus have I had thee as a dream doth flatter—
>   In sleep a king, but waking no such matter.

Here the marketplace tone and the marketplace reasoning are
so insistent as to be unmistakable—and resented. The pun on
"dear" in the first line, for all its obviousness, still manages to
be effective because, in bringing together one meaning from

the world of sentiment and one meaning from the marketplace, it sends forth the two poles that create both the dialectic
and the unity of this poem—indeed of all these poems, singly
and as a group.[6] When we first read "dear," we assume that
it functions in the Petrarchan context of affections (despite
"possessing"), only in retrospect to be shocked by the word
"estimate" and all that follows into recognizing that we have
been taken in, have been sentimental fools insufficiently
aware of how the world really operates and, consequently, of
how the word "dear" must really operate. The unbroken
multiplication of legal and financial terms throughout the
octave shouts almost too loudly the poet's bitterness at having
the one kind of "dear" reduced to the other, at having love's
world of troth reduced to the niggardly world of truth, the
world of faith to the world of fact. He uses his metric to this
end also, with a maddening inexorability. The almost un-
varying use of the feminine ending bestows a sing-song
matter-of-factness to each line, each end-stopped with the
voice dropped. No counter-statement is possible: the figures
speak for themselves. Only lines 2 and 4 in the poem do not
have feminine endings, and even in these the extremely weak
final foot ("estimate," "determinate") gives much the same
effect. Except for the couplet, the other lines all end in the
"ing," either in participle or gerund. And the couplet, despite
the shift, has its own feminine ending.

The marketplace assumption for the poem is that the friend
has given his love only through a miscalculation: either he

---

[6] I cannot deal, here and everywhere, with Shakespeare's manipula-
tions of language without repeating Sigurd Burckhardt's brilliant truism
which I cited earlier for the treatment of language as substantive, or,
in his term, "corporeal": "He [Empson] made us aware that one word
can—and in great poetry commonly does—have *many meanings;* I
would rather insist on the converse, that many meanings can have *one
word*" ("The Poet as Fool and Priest," *ELH,* XXIII [1956], 387). It
seems to me no coincidence that Burckhardt is among the most perceptive of readers of Shakespeare.

underestimated his own worth or overestimated the poet's. In the business of love as of all the world of truth, fair value received for value given is all. The gift of the friend's love to the poet is not justified by truthful assessments of the worth of each, so that the friend may properly withdraw it. The friend now has a just "estimate" of his own worth and the poet's, as he did not have when he made the ill-advised gift. Clearly implied, thanks to the couplet, is the claim that the friend, like the poet, has not been awake to the marketplace facts, that his mistake arose from his own dream—the delusive dream of faith and love—that blinded him to the facts of marketplace truth. And the friend's dreamlike unawareness has allowed the poet his own flattering dream of the truth (troth) he would like and his faith demands.

So the poet has been flattered by both the friend and the dream, while the awakening deprives him of both:

> Thus have I had thee as a dream doth flatter—
> In sleep a king, but waking no such matter.

The couplet barely hints at the conjunction of king, flattery, and golden illusion, which is more fully developed elsewhere (see my earlier comments on Sonnets 114 and 33). Here, as in other cases we have seen where explication is enriched by considering the *Sonnets* as a single body of metaphor, I believe we may borrow from the complete development of an image cluster in one sonnet to fill out the mere allusion to it elsewhere. The lowly poet, in being flattered by the delusive dream of love, was converted into king. As in Sonnet 114, his faithful mind had as its subjects the obedient senses which allowed themselves to be asleep to truth in the flattering service of troth. Now is the rude awakening, as truth—which is here restricted to proper calculation—asserts itself. The awakening is poetically rude too: after the idyllic reminiscence of line 13 and the first two feet of line 14, there is the sharp letdown in the last three feet. First, "In sleep a king," but then a total break aided by the caesura, and finally "but waking no such matter": the total dismissal of everything as the punctured dream with the omnibus prosaism, "no such matter." Is it too much to see the last word, the casually and vaguely uttered "matter," as taking on a precision and becoming something of a pun, since it has resulted from the intrusion of the world of "matter," the materialistic world of the marketplace, upon the fond, more-than-marketplace dream—the dream of a world of faith in which worth is not all, or at least is not to be measured by marketplace values? And is this not another form of Shakespeare's judgment on the unmagical, unyielding mirror, measure of the measurable world that, in its vile wisdom, dares not extend itself? Is it not also his mixed judgment on the wormy modern world with its necessary truths, the late, post-chivalric, pragmatic world that we recognize as the world of that mixed hero, Bolingbroke?[7]

The mention of Bolingbroke may lead us to the possibility that it is rather the beloved of Sonnet 87 who has been the king and who, in the couplet, is deprived of his kingliness by the poet's awakening. The syntax of the couplet would perhaps seem to support this even more bitter reading rather than my earlier one. I have had thee as a dream doth flatter: I have had thee in sleep as a king, but on waking I find you to be no such matter. In succumbing to the table of equivalents, the values, of the marketplace, the friend has lowered himself from the glory he shared with the poet when, despite his greater worth, he accepted with the poet their common dream of faith. According to love's paradoxical propriety, in

[7] In several places in the *Sonnets* Shakespeare delivers his judgment on the fallen modern world as "this ill-wresting world" that "has grown bad" (Sonnet 140). See also, for example, all of the bitter Sonnet 66 and the sadness over a "bankrout" nature in Sonnet 67 (". . . what wealth she had/ In days long since, before these last so bad"). On Bolingbroke, see my essay, "The Dark Generations of *Richard III*," in *Criticism*, I (1959), especially pp. 43–44.

accepting the egalitarianism of love he was truly regal; in now accepting the marketplace estimate of his greater worth, he is "no such matter." Indeed, may it not really be the beloved friend who has suffered the greater fall? And the final word of that final phrase that seems to have been tossed out carelessly, "matter," as material, has all the force and more that I suggested in my earlier reading. For the friend's "matter" has been transformed by the end of the dream and the mutual awakening to marketplace reality, with the mutual revaluation it imposes. The "stuff" that "dreams are made on" has no more stability than the dreams themselves.

In seeing the modern world's wormy devotion to truth as the devotion to appearance, Shakespeare is able to see this truth as deceptive, hypocritical, a rude imitation of the archaic troth that is for him truth eternal. The apparent truth of the world is mere cosmetics, the unnatural artifice that, like all art, as merely imitative, has no substance. Thus Sonnets 67–68:

> Ah, wherefore with infection should he live
> And with his presence grace impiety,
> That sin by him advantage should achieve
> And lace itself with his society?
> Why should false painting imitate his cheek
> And steal dead seeing of his living hue?
> Why should poor beauty indirectly seek
> Roses of shadow, since his rose is true?
> Why should he live, now Nature bankrout is,
> Beggar'd of blood to blush through lively veins?
> For she hath no exchequer now but his,
> And, proud of many, lives upon his gains.
>   O, him she stores, to show what wealth she had
>   In days long since, before these last so bad.

> Thus is his cheek the map of days outworn,
> When beauty liv'd and died as flowers do now,

Before these bastard signs of fair were born
Or durst inhabit on a living brow;
Before the golden tresses of the dead,
The right of sepulchres, were shorn away
To live a second life on second head;
Ere beauty's dead fleece made another gay.
In him those holy antique hours are seen,
Without all ornament, itself and true,
Making no summer of another's green,
Robbing no old to dress his beauty new;
    And him as for a map doth Nature store,
    To show false Art what beauty was of yore.

The friend has become the one remnant of truth eternal, "holy antique" truth, a truth that has abandoned the unworthy world. Instead "false Art" has been producing its unsanctioned copies of it. Hence nature's need to "store" him (Sonnet 67, line 13 and 68, 13) as the sole still living model of truth (troth) for the lifeless artifact to work from.

The opposition between substance and shadow, truth and imitation, is indeed an extension of the opposition between nature and art. "False painting" is the cosmetic copy of his natural cheek, the "roses of shadow" which ape his rose that is "true." But the natural, as the eternally true, has the cyclical immortality we have observed earlier in the open mirror-window of nature as contrasted to the closed mirror (without past or future) of Narcissus. Thus the special sin against nature is metaphorically characterized as making "summer of another's green" (Sonnet 68, line 11). Similarly, "his cheek" is proved to be natural by being "the map of days outworn, / When beauty liv'd and died as flowers do now"; while the modern alternative is found in "these bastard signs of fair." It is once again the language of Sonnets 1–17 that renders this opposition, with "bastard" just the strong word needed to cut off the imitative art from a proper history, from man's communal role in the natural cycle ("liv'd and died as flowers do now"). This unnatural growth, as merely imitative appearance without any truth or substance of its own (even if it is the vile, wise world's only truth), must be seen as dead rather than as live—especially if we recall the special sense of "live" in the "breed" sonnets (as we have seen, for example, in Sonnet 4, line 8: " . . . yet canst not live") as giving life in nature's way. Art's way is here the way of death, the desperate alternative caused by a "bankrout" nature "Beggar'd of blood to blush through lively veins" (Sonnet 67, line 10). Hence line 6 of Sonnet 67 ("And steal dead seeing of his living hue") and the second quatrain of Sonnet 68, where the use of lifeless ornaments for the living ("golden tresses of the dead," "beauty's dead fleece") desecrates the past without allowing a future. The tomb is plundered ("The right of sepulchres") to supply what the womb can no longer afford. How different from the reverent nostalgia for the "holy antique hours" of nature, now distilled to the friend's original and "true" substance. There was no need for art, nor for the Platonic dualism between truth and troth, in the "days outworn," holy and antique, when appearance and substance were one ("itself and true," Sonnet 68, line 10). But now they are united only in the poet's beloved friend, incarnation of this union that transcends the division between the world's dull and lifeless truth and a troth now accessible only to the eye of love's faith. This has indeed become a world which invites, needs, and deserves its Bolingbrokes.

3. STATE, PROPERTY, AND THE
POLITICS OF REASON

As my reference to Bolingbroke reminds us, the vile, wise world of worms is a politic world; and Shakespeare is not likely to overlook the possibilities of metaphorical extension in this direction. His Sonnet 124 realizes them magnificently:

If my dear love were but the child of state,
It might for Fortune's bastard be unfather'd,
As subject to Time's love or to Time's hate,
Weeds among weeds, or flowers with flowers gather'd.
No, it was builded far from accident;
It suffers not in smiling pomp, nor falls
Under the blow of thralled discontent,
Whereto th' inviting time our fashion calls.
It fears not Policy, that heretic
Which works on leases of short-number'd hours,
But all alone stands hugely politic,
That it nor grows with heat nor drowns with show'rs.
   To this I witness call the fools of time,
   Which die for goodness, who have liv'd for crime.

The word "state," central object of the poet's disdain, controls the divergent levels that are rooted in the union of its multiple capacities. Primarily, of course, it functions in the majestic world of sovereignty, the summit of the political hierarchy. But it is a transient "state" which, if sovereign in its day, is still "subject" to (which is to say a subject of) time. And its "child" could be "unfather'd" by "Fortune's bastard," that is, by the unlooked for "natural" son, upstart without lineage or history that chance thrusts upward even as it thrusts downward (see "falls under," lines 6–7) the majestic parent "state," which is now proved to be just as accidental, as unsanctioned, in its earlier ascension. The "child of state," then, is "unfather'd" not only in that it is deprived of "state" (its high estate) as its parent but in that state's permanent claim to legitimate fatherhood is shown as false and presumptuous: it also must have been a bastard of fortune after all, as are all who partake of the political realm in which all is vicissitude and there is no true, uncontingent "state."

But the meaning of "state" is thus spreading out to envelop the contingencies of the human condition, the generic "accident" of line 5. The political language continues, but we see politics as the pure, microcosmic reflection of worldly human life, the distillate of its worldly, wormy nature. The word "state" permits us to join the narrowest political notions in the poem to the broadest sense of worldly life as the politic enterprise: state as majesty and as political entity, state as rank or status, state as condition of being (or rather, for time-bound humanity, condition of becoming). In effect, Shakespeare is demonstrating the sweep of the word's semantic history. He proves the justness of his political metaphor by allowing his language to establish the essential oneness of the several political levels of living. Once again the metaphor is earned totally by moving from similarity to substantive identity: the human condition *is* the political condition. "State" and "accident" are finally one, so that the instabilities of the political condition may be read back into the human state at large—or at least the human state without love, the human state in its narcissistic self-enclosure, the self-interest that exposes it to politics as a universal force.

Of course, the broad universality has been indicated earlier by the shift in lines 3–4 to the unaltering natural process at once capricious and all-inclusive: "Time's love," "Time's hate," "Weeds among weeds or flowers with flowers"—but all equally "gather'd" (with the sickle image clearly implied). Still even this universality must allow the exemption of the poet's "dear love." For this love is not "subject to" the capricious sameness of time. And it is not a "child of state" and is thus free from the consequences of "accident" which universal political bastardy otherwise imposes. Nor is it the victim of "Policy," which as "heretic" is another form of the earlier "bastard," unauthorized violator of wholeness and orderly plan since its very existence denies both. But, as a mystic celebrant of love, the poet has been defining love negatively, in terms of what it is *not*. For the only terms available are those of the world, those antagonistic to love that are mentioned only to have their relations to love denied. When finally in line 11 he makes his sole attempt at a positive definition—completed with more negatives in the following line—he again borrows his crucial term from the antagonistic, loveless world. Indeed, the crowning characteristic he bestows upon love, that it "all alone stands hugely politic," gathers its paradoxical power from the juxtaposition of "hugely politic" to its etymological brother, the despised heretic "Policy" just two lines earlier.

It is a brilliant maneuver. The seeming contradiction is finally persuasive: the only way to be successfully politic is to reject policy altogether, not to be politic at all, to stand alone outside state, fortune, time, accident, pomp, discontent, heat and showers. This only is the way to be totally, absolutely, permanently—"hugely"—politic, the way to destroy the hold of the loveless politic world. Master or slave, the user of policy is finally subject. But to stand like love, all alone and hugely politic, is to evade the domain of master and slave, to be by oneself and sovereign, with absolute power, but only over oneself. Indeed, there is yet another likely meaning to the word "politic": to be "hugely politic" is to constitute oneself as a body politic. And so the self-containedness of love, in all its disdain of and inaccessibility to the terms of the world, constitutes itself a body politic distinct and indissoluble, untouchable by all others and subject to none—

finally beyond the "state" of man (in all its senses) whose child it is not.

Love's sovereign aloneness is enhanced by its contrast with the undiscriminating inclusiveness of the dominion of time which it excludes. We have already seen in line 4 the sudden absorption of man's unelevated political state within the universal state of nature—a nature seen without the immortalizing circularity and thus as time's subject, in its dying cycle only. But as man's state is shown to be the same as that of *all* creation of which he is but a part, so this universal state under time is shown as totally indifferent to that "all" which share in it. "Time's love" or "Time's hate," "weeds" or "flowers," "smiling pomp" or "thralled discontent," "grows with heat" or "drowns with showers"—all is one and it just does not matter, for accident in the time-ridden state makes the alternatives interchangeable and therefore meaningless, as they all come to the same thing. The alternatives (note the use of "or" and "nor") are meant to be polar and exhaustive. There is no other possibility, except for the irrational one of love's transcendence. As the poet has been able to define love only by using the terms of the loveless world, so he can call to witness the truth of his definition only the members of that inadequate world, "the fools of time." This suggests all people but the lovers, so that he must classify these too in polar alternatives, exhaustive and yet utterly futile, as futile as state. Hence the final line, with its opposing pairs and incongruous clauses of cross-purposes:[1] "die" or "have liv'd,"

---

[1] In accordance with the precedents of the earlier use of "or" and "nor" (lines 3, 4, 6, 12), I am of course suggesting that an "or" is understood between the two clauses of line 14, thus allowing them to join and crown the parade of alternatives I have traced. I must ignore the reading that seems more immediately likely and is surely the common one: that the two clauses refer to the same people. Finally this reading seems to me to give far less to the context of the poem, having taken far less from it.

"for goodness" or "for crime"; but, ironically, even cynically, "Which die for goodness," or "who have liv'd for crime."[2] There can be no further witnesses of the extent and foolishness of the time-server and, by negation, of the transcendent power of love.

In Sonnet 64 we have a universalizing of the "accidental" nature of "state" that is more complete and perhaps even more powerful.[3]

> When I have seen by Time's fell hand defaced
> The rich proud cost of outworn buried age;
> When sometime lofty towers I see down rased,
> And brass eternal slave to mortal rage;
> When I have seen the hungry ocean gain
> Advantage on the kingdom of the shore,
> And the firm soil win of the wat'ry main,
> Increasing store with loss, and loss with store;
> When I have seen such interchange of state,
> Or state itself confounded, to decay;
> Ruin hath taught me thus to ruminate,
> That Time will come and take my love away.
> This thought is as a death, which cannot choose
> But weep to have that which it fears to lose.

In moving from the first to the second quatrain, we move from the world of man to the world of nature, from the succession of states to the succession of unending cycles in the rhythmic heart of the universe. Shakespeare begins by observing the destruction of the noblest and most ambitious of human pro-

---

[2] Could it be that Shakespeare varies even his relative pronouns ("Which," "who") to help polarize the two clauses and show them as exhaustive?

[3] The total power of the sonnet can be realized only in conjunction with its sequel in Sonnet 65. But the unified effect of the entire 28-line unit must await later examination since it is centrally relevant to my following chapter. At this point it is only the universalizing of "state" that concerns me.

ductions, with the ironic use of "eternal" (line 4) the clue to his scornful view of human claims to immortality. Even more insulting to the "eternal" is its being at the mercy of that which is itself "mortal." This word "mortal" is the perfect word: first, its juxtaposition to "eternal" inverts the proper relation of master and slave between them; secondly, its implication that the wielders of the rage that destroys the "eternal" are themselves to be destroyed makes them no less the victims of time than are *their* victims; and thirdly, it makes possible the contrast between these "mortal" agents in the first quatrain and the natural, seemingly immortal agents in the second.

But as if to prove the claim that the human political state is a microcosmic reflection of the universal state of time, the antagonists of the second quatrain, the ocean and the shore, are rendered totally in human terms, as they act in accordance with political motives. Thus the apparent distinction between the human and the natural in the two quatrains is methodically blurred. As we have seen in Sonnet 124, all the realms of "state" have been identified and reduced to the extreme consequences of the narrowest meaning, that of human politics.[4] As in Sonnet 124, the one word, despite its range of meanings, from narrow to broad, is shown to be a single reductive entity that can contain and unite them all even within its narrowest confines. For these can be extended unlimitedly without losing their most precise limitations—just the test of the sound metaphor. In Sonnet 64 the extension into nature is even more remarkable.

The ocean, seen as "hungry" for acquisition of another's, is at once the greedy state and the insatiable worm. But it reduces "the kingdom of the shore" only later to be forced to

---

[4] The tactic seems similar to the one I described in my discussion of Sonnet 71 ("No longer mourn for me when I am dead"), where Shakespeare was seen to turn the wise, vile world into a less extreme version of its purest representatives, the vilest worms.

give back what it has gained along with some of its own. He who feeds like a worm shall be fed upon by another. Like Matthew Arnold's "ignorant armies" on Dover Beach several centuries later, these clash futilely and endlessly with none but temporary victories that give way to later defeats, just as temporary.[5] Thus the inconclusive "interchange of state" (line 9) or, in terms that suggest the first quatrain, "state itself confounded to decay" (line 10), as the political sense of state achieves its universal sway under time, incorporating the other senses. The many politic antagonists can only interchange their states, as his metaphor enables Shakespeare's human and natural antagonists to interchange *their* states. And all are on their way to eventual destruction. Thus, in the first two lines of the sequel, Sonnet 65, which summarize these two quatrains of Sonnet 64,

> Since brass, nor stone, nor earth, nor boundless sea,
> But sad mortality o'ersways their power,

Shakespeare can join all the forces, the results of human and natural agents, and characterize them all as subject to "mortality." So none should have any more pretension to being "eternal" than did the brass (Sonnet 64, line 4) and all, by implication, are equally victims of one or another sort of "mortal rage." The human term "mortality" succeeds in reducing the entire material universe, as a struggling, politic, loveless state, to the state of being time's fool.

The fool of time appears again in Sonnet 116, and, as in Sonnet 124, love is exempt from this state.

> Let me not to the marriage of true minds
> Admit impediments. Love is not love
> Which alters when it alteration finds
> Or bends with the remover to remove.

[5] The extent to which this sense is the controlling one in *Dover Beach* is shown in my essay, "*Dover Beach* and the Tragic Sense of Eternal Recurrence," *University of Kansas City Review*, XXIII (1956), 73–79.

O, no! it is an ever-fixed mark
That looks on tempests and is never shaken;
It is the star to every wand'ring bark,
Whose worth's unknown, although his highth be taken
Love's not Time's fool, though rosy lips and cheeks
Within his bending sickle's compass come.
Love alters not with his brief hours and weeks,
But bears it out even to the edge of doom.
      If this be error, and upon me proved,
      I never writ, nor no man ever loved.

Love as "the marriage of true minds" reminds us that we are
in the world of troth. Thus there must be no "impediments"
to this marriage since only a subject of time can be forced to
cooperate with time to produce an impediment. The cooperation with time is verbally enforced by the effective repetition
that has time's fool following upon the aging action ("alters
when it alteration finds") and the destructive action ("bends
with the remover to remove") of time and his sickle.[6] The
seconding action this repetition suggests is especially persuasive in contrast to the use of repetition, joined by "not,"
in order to negate—even expunge—in the preceding line
("Love is not love"). There is the further repetition of forms
of "bend" and "alter" in lines 10 and 11, giving a reverse or
mirror-image of lines 3 and 4 (and, among other things,

---

[6] There is ample precedent in the *Sonnets* for both alteration by age
and removal by death to be caused by time's sickle or scythe. I quote
again the third quatrain of Sonnet 60:

> Time doth transfix the flourish set on youth
> And delves the parallels in beauty's brow,
> Feeds on the rarities of nature's truth,
> And nothing stands but for his scythe to mow . . .

It would seem to enforce the reading of lines 3 and 4 of Sonnet 116 as
implying the reaper once more, especially in view of the motion indicated by "bends" and the fact that the motion is echoed in the "bending
sickle's compass" of line 10, where the reaping stroke of time is made
explicit.

reinforcing the sickle image of line 4).[7] The third quatrain, as an intensified echo of the first, presses the negative definition of love, of which we have seen a more sustained instance in Sonnet 124. Love will not add its destruction to that of the "rosy lips and cheeks," but rather asserts its eternal fixity.[8] Here in the third quatrain, as in the echoes of lines 3 and 4, we are once more in the world of Sonnet 71 (and the line, "But let your love even with my life decay"). This reminds us of the opposition between truth and troth, time's truth and love's. As we have seen in the preceding chapters, love is outside the world of Narcissus and his linear time, since to be inside is to become its subject and agent as are the worms. So it is not surprising that, when Shakespeare does

[7] In view of the central importance to these sonnets of time and the sweep of his sickle, I cannot agree with those commentators who read "compass" as having, even secondarily, any relation to the "wand'ring bark" image of line 7. There is nothing in the context of line 10 to support a nautical reading, and the context of the poem hardly seems to require it or benefit from it, so that such a reading would seem to suggest only an uninhibited, laissez-faire hunt for double-meaning anywhere it can be found.

[8] Here Shakespeare's Christianity makes some trouble for his Platonism. Line 12, "But bears it out even to the edge of doom," inconsistently imposes a limitation of time upon love—however generous—that would after all keep love as time's child, though its most long-lived one. The Christian break between time and timelessness, marked by the last judgment, intrudes upon the eternal perfection of love to make it less than infinite. Shakespeare's metaphorical dedication to love's totally sovereign timelessness should force it to elude the domain of Christian time and timelessness. And "doom" can of course have no other meaning than doomsday. See, for example, the final lines of Sonnet 55, where Shakespeare works out the conflict between the two eternities far more successfully, perhaps because he is there dealing with a person rather than with love as an entity, a mystic union:

> 'Gainst death and all-oblivious enmity
> Shall you pace forth; your praise shall still find room
> Even in the eyes of all posterity
> That wear this world out to the ending doom.
>> So, till the judgment that yourself arise,
>> You live in this, and dwell in lovers' eyes.

introduce a positive definition in the second quatrain,[9] he insists on a value for the star beyond the futile measurability of fact: "Whose worth's unknown, although his highth be taken." His extravagance—anti-scientific, may we call it?—is of course beyond logic as well as fact. Yet, as if in defiance of logic and fact, the unreasonable reason of love asserts its own version of logic and fact in the pseudo-syllogism of the couplet. The fact is the existence of this very sonnet, which is to prove that the poet has indeed "writ." The tactic here may remind us of the argumentative factuality of the "this" in Sonnet 74, lines 5–6 ("When thou reviewest this, thou dost review / The very part was consecrate to thee") and the couplet ("The worth of that is that which it contains, / And that is this, and this with thee remains"), which I have discussed earlier in these terms. The logic there is similar too: the fact of this poem is guarantor of the poet's faith ("the very part was consecrate to thee"), of the immaterial "spirit," and of his true (that is, trothful) "worth."

Here, in Sonnet 116, the fact of his having written is the proof of his having loved. Love's faith is constituted by the poem, the one mirror-window testifying to the other. The testament of love is the embassy of poetry. As an aesthetically successful mirror-window, the sovereign entity which is the poem is "hugely politic," the body politic of Sonnet 124, which becomes the material proof as it is the domain, the physical realm, of love. Yet, together with love, it is exempt from man's "state" so that it too is no fool of time. Thus in Sonnet 116, as in Sonnet 74 and elsewhere, Shakespeare does more than borrow the Petrarchan convention of defying mortality through verse: by using the fact of this poem he matches the materialism of mortality and its truth with the

---

[9] Here he is using a different strategy from what we have seen in Sonnet 124. He makes a positive claim and makes it in terms most unrelated to his negative claims, but he can do so only by leaping to an extravagant metaphor borrowed from a common Petrarchan conceit.

materialism of immortality and its troth, with verse—the spirit made word and thing—the incarnation and thus the living proof of the immaterial world. The confident, absolute tone of the couplet is further ensured by the unqualified opposites of eternity, "never" and "ever," especially as these repeat the earlier opposition between them in lines 5 and 6. But nothing less absolute can do for the pure logic of love's reason, with its total identity of faith and the word, of faith *in* the word.

Shakespeare dedicated one of his most brilliant poems to the celebration of love's unreasonable reason. I refer, of course, to *The Phoenix and Turtle*. I believe it would not really be a digression for me to pause and touch upon it here. In dealing with this difficult poem, I mean only to indicate briefly its corroboration and extension of what I have been finding in the *Sonnets*. We can begin with the opposition between the birds in the first two stanzas that echoes the various forms of the opposition I have traced from the start. Here it is betweeen the chaste, calm purity of true love that later becomes its own womb and the consuming heat of destructive gratification that is its own tomb. As "augur of the fever's end," this latter bird leads to Yeats's "fury and the mire of human veins." As "foul precurrer of the fiend," it represents a living (though self-destructive) hell.

But the poem turns totally from this pole, dwelled upon extensively elsewhere—and everywhere in the *Sonnets*—to the cool assurances of troth:

> Love and constancy is dead,
> Phoenix and the turtle fled
> In a mutual flame from hence.
>
> (Stanza 6)

The seemingly ungrammatical singular verb "is" is crucial here, of course. It emphasizes, as does the "mutual flame," love's essential oneness: in the language of the following stanza, though "they lov'd as love in twain / Had the essence but in one." Shakespeare continues, "Two distincts, division none: / Number there in love was slain." The apparent distinctness decreed by the law of identity, central to the operation of human reason, is declared abrogated, so that "number" is "slain" "in love."

Number is destroyed in several ways: in finding but one where there seemed to be two, a single number has been lost or destroyed through the union of love; but, further, number has been wiped out altogether, since we are reduced to the number one from the number two, and one is no number at all (we should recall Sonnet 136, lines 7–8: "In things of great receipt with ease we prove / Among a number one is reckon'd none"). But primarily, once the loss of the distinctness of number is involved in the flat contradiction of line 27, that there are both "two distincts" and "division none," this loss must involve the destruction of the very concept of number as an operative instrument.

With the simple logic of primary mathematics thus set aside, further contradictions follow, as the next two lines also contain two incompatible parts each, both firmly asserted: their "hearts" are at once both "remote, yet not asunder"; between them there is "distance," and yet "no space is seen." Surely the poet is justified in proclaiming that "in them it were a wonder"—the miraculous wonder of love's troth that in this poem is seen to exist side by side with the world's dull, limiting truth which it contradicts and, in more than one sense of the word, confounds.

> Property was thus appalled,
> That the self was not the same;
> Single nature's double name
> Neither two nor one was called.
>
> Reason, in itself confounded,
> Saw division grow together,

To themselves yet either neither,
Simple were so well compounded;
That it cried, "How true a twain
Seemeth this concordant one!
Love hath reason, reason none,
If what parts can so remain."

The destruction of number of course implies the destruction of "property." As one's distinctness or identity is lost, so necessarily is the very notion of property, the defining characteristic of an entity, that which belongs to it and makes it what it is.[10] But if what one is is no longer distinct, if one's outer bounds and limitations are overrun and become commingled with another's, thus obliterating the barrier between oneness or selfhood and otherness, then how can "property" be secure? how can it be anything but "appalled"? And can we not easily extend the line from "property," the characteristic that defines and belongs to an entity, to "property," that which is possessed by someone for his use? Does not Shakespeare's use of this word give it a range like that we earlier allowed to "state"? Can we not see a controlling meaning that unites the broad, logical sense of "property" to its narrower economic sense? From the first of the *Sonnets* we have seen how love's mirror, in turning window, breaks the seal, the self-enclosed tomb of the unmagical mirror of Narcissus, which is the measure of the self-interested world's truth. Here, in breaking the distinctness of entity, in threatening the world of number and logic, love threatens the world of property, that which one owns, that which one exploits to serve his own interest. And as we saw "state" reduce man's

[10] Here again, in the defiance of "property," we find Shakespeare fighting also, if secondarily, for the kind of substantive metaphor I have been working toward from the start. For this defiance is a justification of Shakespeare's poetic method, his creation of union in metaphor, as well as of his poetic substance, the union in love he celebrates.

generic state to his political state, so here "property" reduces man's property as a defined being to his property as an owning being. As state reduced man's reality under time to his political reality, so property reduces man's identity as an isolated individual to his economic identity. To man's reality as politic we add the further materializing qualification that it is self-interestedly economic. The world opposed to love is debased further.

Of course, it is reason, in its untranscendental sense, that is queen and arbiter of the loveless world. But "confounded" by the "wonder" of love's destruction of number and property, reason must itself testify to its own powerlessness in the face of miracle. With the line, "Love hath reason, reason none," reason in effect abdicates to the higher unreasonable reason which it cannot comprehend and with which it cannot co-exist. And, as the final irony, reason becomes composer of the Threnos, the chorus that accompanies as it celebrates the phenomenon that has dethroned it.

Nevertheless, it is reason alone that seems to be left to this world. It is as if Shakespeare is providing evidence for the claim that the archaic world of troth has abandoned our world to the literalistic truth of appearance; that the reason which the pragmatic world worships rules only as a consequence of the withdrawal of that which demonstrates its inadequacy; and that, in the face of love, which is the only extant evidence of the world of faith and faith's reason, reason itself—the reason of number and property—acknowledges its shabbiness.

> Truth may seem, but cannot be;
> Beauty brag, but 'tis not she:
> Truth and Beauty buried be.
>
> To this urn let those repair
> That are either true or fair;
> For these dead birds sigh a prayer.

Only seeming truth remains with us in our world, along with an imitation of beauty.[11] Truth itself (the truth that can "be") is buried with beauty, although theirs is an immortality beyond our world. Still it renders its critique of this world and beckons those "either true or fair" who would turn aside from false truth and beauty to emulate the Phoenix and Turtle and achieve their resurrection. For the rest, reason alone is left to the deserted, fallen world as its ruler even though it has abdicated its right to rule by acknowledging all that it cannot account for. For the loveless world cannot call it to this account.

Thus in the one poem reason denies itself and yields to love, while acting as the chorus to love's death from the now fallen world, the death that ensures the continued reign of reason even as it corroborates reason's derogation of itself by showing reason to be master only of apparent truth and imitative beauty. The miracle of love's union, even in its withdrawal from the common world, still towers above reason, accessible to love's mystic. Among many places in the *Sonnets* in which Shakespeare struggles to earn his claim to the miracle's presence is the curious and unique group of Sonnets 33–39. In the implied narrative sequence in these poems, the poet shows himself most impolitic, the antithesis of what he urges his friend to be in Sonnet 71 ("No longer mourn for me"), as he fights to destroy apparent truth, even the truth about the commission of sin. The group traces a circular dialectic. The poet starts with a most disappointed awareness of the friend's crime, then tries to excuse it, sees this attempt as a greater crime of his own, thus takes the guilt upon himself, and ends this inversion by pleading with the now guiltless friend

---

[11] I recall my discussion at the close of the preceding chapter of the contrast between the original true beauty, holy and antique, of a now "bankrout nature" and the "bastard signs" of imitation in Sonnets 67–68. There too we were given the sense of having come upon bad days. These lines in *The Phoenix and Turtle* seem to create the mythic framework for the historical implications of these sonnets.

to avoid so darkened a creature as the poet. As reward, his sacrifice has earned an essential union with the friend that allows the poet to share his glory as his own.

Sonnet 33 begins the sequence by acknowledging the moral darkening of his glorious friend, rendered—and in part justified—by the image of the sovereign sun (which I discussed earlier in relation to Sonnets 114 and 87) disgracefully eclipsed by "basest clouds." Using the darkening of "heaven's sun" as his excuse, the poet urges the constancy of his love despite the darkening of *his* sun, the friend. It is his constant love that authorizes what he does for the friend in the sequel.

Sonnet 34 has the quality of dialectic that characterizes this entire sequence. The poet first rebukes the friend for surprising and disappointing him, still using the analogy of sun and clouds from Sonnet 33. Nor can the friend's repentant attempt to "dry the rain" on the poet's face cure "the disgrace." But the poet finally joins him in search for a way out of the consequences of the sin. One metaphor is tried after another to dissolve the offense. From the rain as "salve" to heal the "wound," to "shame" as "physic" for "grief," to repentance as relief for the poet's burden. But the last may open the way for the poet to find an escape:

> Th' offender's sorrow lends but weak relief
> To him that bears the strong offence's cross.
>
> (lines 11–12)

The final word, "cross," promises more than we should have expected from the negative force of these lines which in this seem to resemble those that preceded it. With this word we have not only the prospect of the poet, as innocent, taking the sin upon himself, but also the introduction of hope, of the chance for ransom, for redemption. We are ready for the couplet which fulfills that hope, if recklessly so:

> Ah, but those tears are pearl which thy love sheeds,
> And they are rich and ransom all ill deeds.

Finally this metaphor works the trick, if only by fiat. The "Ah" suggests the sudden, surprising discovery of the specious opening that the metaphor in the couplet offers him. The poet leaps to grasp the unearned transfer from "tears" to "pearl" to "ransom" which appears to solve his problem only at an unsubstantive level of language. Are we to see him as permitting himself to be deceived by his language in his desperation to exonerate his friend? And may this not be part of the poet's sin that he makes explicit in the second quatrain of the following sonnet? Still there is the sense in which "ransom" does fulfill the expectations of "cross." It may rather be that the very unearned conclusion of this metaphor is in keeping with the miraculous nature of the "ransom" in the wake of the "cross."

But is it not finally the poet who, as bearer of the "cross" still, is finally to pay the cost of this ransom, empowered as he is by the friend's love indicated by his tears? So there is no miracle in that no absolution is without price. Neither the poet's burden nor his sorrow is actually relieved, despite the verbal satisfaction of the couplet. The following sonnets prove it. The very next opens with the plea that the friend no longer be burdened by his sin, for this sonnet is the very process of the poet's ransoming him at the cost of his own innocence.

No more be griev'd at that which thou hast done:
Roses have thorns, and silver fountains mud;
Clouds and eclipses stain both moon and sun,
And loathsome canker lives in sweetest bud.
All men make faults, and even I in this,
Authorizing thy trespass with compare,
Myself corrupting, salving thy amiss,
Excusing thy sins more than thy sins are;
For to thy sensual fault I bring in sense—
Thy adverse party is thy advocate—

And 'gainst myself a lawful plea commence.
Such civil war is in my love and hate
　That I an accessary needs must be
　To that sweet thief which sourly robs from me.

Let me confess that we two must be twain,
Although our undivided loves are one.
So shall those blots that do with me remain,
Without thy help by me be borne alone.
In our two loves there is but one respect,
Though in our lives a separable spite,
Which though it alter not love's sole effect,
Yet doth it steal sweet hours from love's delight.
I may not evermore acknowledge thee,
Lest my bewailed guilt should do thee shame;
Nor thou with public kindness honour me,
Unless thou take that honour from thy name.
　But do not so. I love thee in such sort
　As, thou being mine, mine is thy good report.

The comparison in the first quatrain of Sonnet 35 recalls
us to the poet's analogical excuse for his friend in the first of
this group, Sonnet 33, with line 3 echoing the sun-cloud image
on which Sonnet 33 was based. But by now, having taken us
through the desperate search for the metaphorical ransom in
Sonnet 34, and having gotten us there by way of the "cross,"
the poet must draw moral conclusions about what his love
for his friend has caused him to do. Thus the second quatrain
and all that follows it: the very comparisons, in authorizing
the "trespass," testify to the poet's "fault."

The tactic of self-accusation is brilliant: first he shows the
friend's fault to be like the necessary imperfections in nature;
then he claims it shows a fallibility common to all men; then
he applies this general proposition about human fallibility
to himself as a man, proving his claim by pointing to this very
sonnet and his attempt in it to justify his friend's fault "with

compare"; finally, he gets lost in the contemplation of his own complicity in sin, even though the poem's rhetoric originally had him offering himself as a mere example of human imperfection. He allows the dialectic to carry him on finally (in Sonnet 36) to the total exoneration of the friend and the total condemnation of himself. Line 7 of Sonnet 35 ends by having quite literal consequences. The poet *has* corrupted himself in "salving" the friend's "amiss." He is now seriously infected as the friend's "amiss" is completely cured. The "physic" worked for the moral patient, and the too anxious physician is left with the moral ailment, stricken by this very physic, and beyond help.

After the grammatical and textual confusions of line 8 (although there seems to be no doubt about its general meaning), line 9 strikes profoundly: "To thy sensual fault I bring in sense." The play on "sense" here is as serious and as significant as Donne's play on it in relation to "absence" in the lines from *A Valediction Forbidding Mourning* that I have discussed earlier. The poet has been using "sense" (as reasonable argument, good sense) to transform the friend's "sensual fault" into something else. This is, in effect, like reason playing "the bawd to lust's abuse" in the lines from *Venus and Adonis* I cited in another connection. This perversion of Lord Reason's proper function is sin enough, for it changes reason into a changeling, into a subordinate and renegade form of lust. But Shakespeare's language forces the opposition between right reason and lust to fade into something close to identity between them. "Sensual fault" and "sense," the same or opposite?—especially when "sense" cannot help but have its other meaning, related to desire, rub off on its intellectual, more austere meaning. Or is it more austere? Can it be when the very word has an ambivalence that can hardly be accidental, in view of how this sonnet is proving it? This phonetic echo ("sensual," "sense") that threatens, in becoming substantive, to destroy opposition, leads to other echoes and to the unhappy identity the poem earns between "adverse" and "advocate" and "sweet" and "sourly" (as well as, without echo, "love" and "hate"), made one by the crucial "accessary," the word that tells us the explicit nature of the charge against the poet.

By Sonnet 36 the transfer of guilt has worked. It has become so concentrated in the poet it corrupted that it seems to be only in him. As bearer of "the strong offence's cross," he has taken it all on himself, leaving the friend with "honour" (line 12), "worth and truth" (Sonnet 37, line 4), and even "glory" (Sonnet 37, line 12). For "those blots that do with me remain," he faithfully promises, "without thy help by me be borne alone." And so it is, thanks to his "bewailed guilt." Now it is the friend who must avoid the poet, to keep his newly purified self uncorrupted by the transferred, corrupting guilt. Of course, by Sonnet 36 it is the reputation of sin in the eyes of the world, rather than sin itself, that is at stake—although the poet, in his selfless generosity, never suggests that the moral reputation and true moral worth are unjustly paired. For he accepts the friend's absolution and never questions the justness of his own dishonor. So the language of Sonnet 36, as later of Sonnet 39, is that of *The Phoenix and Turtle,* with the paradoxical simultaneity of oneness and duality, union and division. By Sonnet 39, this leads to the separation theme (begun with the "separable spite" of Sonnet 36) that is in many ways parallel to Donne's handling of physical separation in *A Valediction Forbidding Mourning.* The seeming duality of the poet and his friend is accentuated by the vastness of the ground separating their moral positions, especially in the eyes of the world. For the sake of the friend's honor the "two must be twain." Indeed, it is their twain-ness that enabled the poet to assume the guilt alone and to permit his friend his "good report." But as in *The Phoenix and Turtle,* the two are essentially one and "undivided" despite whatever separates them. The proof is in these poems: the poet can totally assume the guilt, though it began as the friend's, and he—though lowly and dishonored—can thoroughly share the glory that is the friend's, thanks to his sacrifice. So again Shakespeare has it both ways: he exploits their separateness to allow the poet to absolve the friend of guilt that started as his alone, and he exploits their union to allow the poet to be one with the friend in the glory that has been secured for him. As reward for his sacrifice, the poet—through the oneness he has earned by taking another's sin as his own—gains back all he has given up and more. His assumption of guilt has destroyed this otherness, and all the friend's advantages become his too. The world's "spite" is small price for this victory over its truth and niggardly distinctions. Once more the opening mirror—the mirror-window—has triumphed over the closed mirror of Narcissus.

It is through this sacrifice and winning back, through this assumption of guilt that ends by being an assumption of glory, that this sequence of poems comes to stand as an effective case for the operation of love's unreasonable reason, as it is asserted in *The Phoenix and Turtle*. The affirmation of the effects of union starts mildly enough in the couplet of Sonnet 36: "But do not so. I love thee in such sort / As, thou being mine, mine is thy good report."[12] Sonnet 37 strengthens the claim:

> As a decrepit father takes delight
> To see his active child do deeds of youth,
> So I, made lame by Fortune's dearest spite,
> Take all my comfort of thy worth and truth . . .

The simile is specially relevant in more than one way. The poet, in making himself "decrepit," *has* fathered the friend,

---

[12] This couplet is identical with that of Sonnet 96, indicating, of course, a confusion in the text. But I think it is clear that the couplet is far more in keeping with the context of Sonnet 36 so that the error is more likely in the other sonnet.

has created him afresh and innocent as his "active child," in whose worth he can share. The early "breed" sonnets should remind us that we cannot take the simile of parentage lightly. We have seen that the son, as mirror-window, is a second coming of the father and one in essence with him. It is thus an ideal vehicle for that other mirror-window created in the beloved, and gives flesh to it.

When, later in this sonnet, Shakespeare introduces the shadow-substance conceit, he is using other terms for the mirror-window—and terms less successful in lending themselves to consistent development.[13]

> For whether beauty, birth, or wealth, or wit,
> Or any of these all, or all, or more,
> Entitled in thy parts do crowned sit,
> I make my love engrafted to this store.
> So then I am not lame, poor, nor despis'd
> Whilst that this shadow doth such substance give
> That I in thy abundance am suffic'd
> And by a part of all thy glory live.

Here is surely another version of the mirror-window paradox. The lamed poet finds his consoling joy by living in the shadow of his friend's glory, but finds that he is fully part of that glory, so that what seems shadow is finally substance too. He is literally "engrafted" to the friend's "store," can share his living substance and his growth. The poet is richer than he could have been without his sacrifice, since he has allowed the more lordly of this unified pair to remain pure. It is in this sense that he has gained more than he gave away, for the poet now shares in attributes of the friend, related to his high birth, to which he could never have laid claim, except for the fruits of the miraculous union which his sacrifice has

[13] A more extended and successful use of shadow and substance occurs in Sonnet 53 ("What is your substance, whereof are you made"), which will enter this discussion in the next chapter.

produced. So by this point in the sequence of sonnets the poet has considerably strengthened his claim to the extensive consequences of the lovers' union ("That I in thy abundance am suffic'd / And by a part of all thy glory live").

To the two mirror-windows of union—in and through pro-creation and in and through love—that Shakespeare joined in the first quatrain of Sonnet 37, he adds a third, poetry, as their further reflection in Sonnets 38 and 39. The union is extended even more. For the very value of the friend, achieved through the devaluing of the poet and enhanced by their separation, is one with the value of the poetry ("While thou dost breathe, that pour'st into my verse / Thine own sweet argument"). The internal phonetic pattern of the last line of Sonnet 38 reflects the union of the absent subject and the present poem, of his heights and the poet's depths:

> If my slight Muse do please these curious days,
> The pain be mine, but thine shall be the praise.

The alliteration and assonance between "pain" and "praise," as combined with the "mine"—"thine" internal rhyme, achieve both the polarity and identity of the two. But it is Sonnet 39 which develops the present-absent, worthless-worthy themes to their completion, as the poet's repayment for his sacrifice is made in full, thanks to the Phoenix paradox which the sacrifice has made operative in the world:

> O, how thy worth with manners may I sing
> When thou art all the better part of me?
> What can mine own praise to mine own self bring?
> And what is't but mine own when I praise thee?
> Even for this let us divided live
> And our dear love lose name of single one,
> That by this separation I may give
> That due to thee which thou deserv'st alone.
> O absence, what a torment wouldst thou prove,

Were it not thy sour leisure gave sweet leave
To entertain the time with thoughts of love,
Which time and thoughts so sweetly doth deceive,
    And that thou teachest how to make one twain—
    By praising him here who doth hence remain!

The strongest affirmation of union is made in the couplet, because it is affirmed in the presence of duality, a duality that has been proved to be both specious and tactically useful. It fools the world of appearance in order to persuade it of the higher truth of the friend's value. Thus, after the assertion of union in the first quatrain (especially lines 2 and 4), the poet reveals his scheme: the seeming separation before the world will permit me to praise you as I could not in propriety praise myself; and, for all its sorrow, your absence is both a joy and a blessing to my poetry and its estimate of your worth. That worth is finally one with the poet's, as the existence of the poem proves, despite the surface deception that suggests a separation between the poet and his subject ("By praising him here who doth hence remain!"). Lo, there is no absence after all for love's (and poetry's) unreasonable reason—no more here than in Donne's *A Valediction Forbidding Mourning*. And in the sequence beginning with Sonnet 33, Shakespeare's dialectic of sin, ransom, sacrifice, and reward through union has earned the heights of his Platonic denial of the apparent distinctness of entities.

The fruits that this union has entitled the poet to claim appear in many places, with Sonnet 62 a splendid example:

Sin of self-love possesseth all mine eye
And all my soul and all my every part;
And for this sin there is no remedy,
It is so grounded inward in my heart.
Methinks no face so gracious is as mine,
No shape so true, no truth of such account,
And for myself mine own worth do define

As I all other in all worths surmount.
But when my glass shows me myself indeed,
Beated and chopt with tann'd antiquity,
Mine own self-love quite contrary I read;
Self so self-loving were iniquity.
      'Tis thee (myself) that for myself I praise,
      Painting my age with beauty of thy days.

Here, in the self-praise which is other-praise, we have the triumph of union over separation in accordance with the tactics indicated in Sonnet 39. In Sonnets 67–68, with which I concluded my last chapter, Shakespeare condemns the "bastard signs of fair," that come from using another's beauty to enhance one's own. For these constitute imitative beauty, mere "roses of shadow." But this condemnation cannot extend to the poet in Sonnet 62, though he admittedly paints his age with the friend's beauty, since his use—springing from love's union—is not imitative. For the two are one. The high opinion that the poet has of himself in the octave he has in spite of his unmagical mirror; the high opinion is justified in the couplet through the magical mirror of his friend who, in their union, is both another and the poet himself. With the transforming cosmetic of the younger friend, we see the simile of Sonnet 37 as surely applicable here: the poet is a "decrepit father" rejuvenated by his "active child," as again the two mirror-windows created by affection and parenthood are seen as one. Love here does for the aging, "beated and chopt" poet precisely what we have seen "breed" do in the earliest sonnets. In opening the mirror outward, it has destroyed his limited identity for an enlarged and renewed identity that transcends, as it "confounds," the human state, its property, and its politic reason.

4. THE MIRACLE
OF LOVE'S ESCHATOLOGY AND
INCARNATION

MUCH of this final movement in Shakespeare's metaphorical system has been anticipated in what has gone before. From the beginning, in seeing the beloved's eye as at once mirror of the lover and window to the heart, or the child as at once mirror of the past and window to the future, we have been viewing the operation of the miracle that destroys distinctness, the miracle that love uses to create otherness as a substantive extension of selfhood. We have seen that the two mirror-windows are essentially one; that the substantive image in the heart of one's beloved—conveyed in and through the eyes—is finally one with its literal and fleshly creation (or re-creation?) in the child of love, so that the conceit of Sonnet 24 ("Mine eye hath played the painter") and the conceit of Sonnet 3 ("Look in thy glass and tell the face thou viewest") are at bottom the same conceit. Both are miraculously incarnating. Indeed, the special value of joining the two mirror-windows as Shakespeare does in the *Sonnets* (and sometimes, as in Sonnet 37, in a single sonnet) is that the realization of body in the child makes it the material projection and thus evidence of the fanciful equation of the beloved's image in the reflecting eye and the containing heart. Were it not for the Platonic chastity of Shakespeare's "love," we could claim to see the spiritual incarnation in the heart as father and archetype of the physical incarnation in the child of marital love.

The same conceit would allow us to trace this lineage back and higher to its source, to the source of all lineage. For man as the child of God can be seen as *His* substantive reflection. Thus, as in J. V. Cunningham's convincing gloss of man's "glassy essence" (*Measure for Measure*, 2.2.120),[1] man's very creation and nature partake of the paradoxical union of mirror and window. "His glassy essence," as in Scholastic tradition, makes man at once an incarnate entity and a mere image that reflects God. Thus it is his very essence to be led beyond himself while remaining himself; and so he *is* led as he initiates his own mirror-windows of love and of procreation, as if in imitation of God's original creation of him as His mirror-window.[2]

Man's genealogy itself, then, depends on the miracle initiated by His miraculous creation. And it is man's subsequent miracles we have been tracing. To the miraculous transfers of love and of procreation (and, metaphorically, of poetry), which I traced in my first chapter on the *Sonnets,* we have seen in subsequent chapters Shakespeare add the miraculous transformations of troth that free it from the wormy world of truth, and the miraculous transcendence of a union that overrides the lower reason of state and property and their politic realm. The latter, of course, in their dull materiality, their ponderousness, continue to assert their sway by offering their heavy resistance—as in the destruction of the trothful dream in Sonnet 87 ("Thus have I had thee as a dream doth flatter —/ In sleep a king, but waking no such matter") or in the poet's insistent, if ironic, yielding to worldly truth in Sonnets 71–72, or in the acknowledgment of the necessity for separateness, even absence, between the lovers in Sonnets 36–39.

The dead weight of the material world and the fleet airiness

---

[1] *Tradition and Poetic Structure* (Denver, 1960), pp. 76–78. He rejects the usual reading of "glassy" as brittle or clear for its more literal meaning of mirrored—thus man's essence as "image of God." Cunningham's entire chapter, with its use of the analogy to the Trinity, is most helpful in defining the precise sort of unreasonable reason revealed in *The Phoenix and Turtle.*

[2] And, more sublimely, in imitation of God's creation of His one Son in the divine perfection of the union of "distincts," the Christian Trinity, as Cunningham reminds us (see especially pp. 83–89).

of the immaterial are most effectively rendered in Shakespeare's use of the four elements in Sonnets 44–45:

> If the dull substance of my flesh were thought,
> Injurious distance should not stop my way;
> For then, despite of space, I would be brought,
> From limits far remote, where thou dost stay.
> No matter then although my foot did stand
> Upon the farthest earth remov'd from thee;
> For nimble thought can jump both sea and land
> As soon as think the place where he would be.
> But, ah, thought kills me that I am not thought,
> To leap large lengths of miles when thou art gone,
> But that, so much of earth and water wrought,
> I must attend time's leisure with my moan,
>   Receiving naught by elements so slow
>   But heavy tears, badges of either's woe.
>
> The other two, slight air and purging fire,
> Are both with thee, wherever I abide;
> The first my thought, the other my desire,
> These present-absent with swift motion slide.
> For when these quicker elements are gone
> In tender embassy of love to thee,
> My life, being made of four, with two alone
> Sinks down to death, oppress'd with melancholy;
> Until life's composition be recured
> By those swift messengers return'd from thee,
> Who even but now come back again, assured
> Of thy fair health, recounting it to me.
>   This told, I joy; but then no longer glad,
>   I send them back again and straight grow sad.

In these we see many of the themes we have seen elsewhere
(for example, the transcendence of space in the "present-absent" "quicker elements"); but I quote them here to show

how Shakespeare uses the oppressive, sinking heaviness of substance as the persistent obstacle to the miraculous, immediate transcendence of substance, as he extends his metaphor through many levels of the Petrarchan conceit toward the conflict between death and life. Thus he can take advantage of the pun on "quick" as both swift and alive, in order to oppose it to the "heavy" elements of earth and water (flesh and tears) as both "slow" and dead. The immaterial, being "quick," is live in a way that leaves only "death" for burdensome matter.

The desperate postulation of miracle—the more desperate for the skepticism engendered by the world, with its obstinate, heavy matter and its modern truth—must continue to be urged in order to avoid the surrender to Narcissus and his tomb. Perhaps the most efficient way of summarizing this postulation is to return to Sonnet 64 ("When I have seen by Time's fell hand defaced") in order to trace its conclusion in Sonnet 65.

Earlier I traced the first two "When" quatrains to their summary in lines 9–10 ("When I have seen such interchange of state, / Or state itself confounded, to decay"), and to the establishment of the fickle dominion of "state" over all of man and nature. The rest of the third quatrain supplies the obvious unhappy consequence for the poet's love of this total dominion: the love too must be subject to time ("Ruin hath taught me thus to ruminate / That Time will come and take my love away"). The comedown from the cosmic and universal to the poet's utterly personal, private concern is startling. After the impressive breadth of the first ten lines and the all-inclusive "ruin" of line 11, the small and helpless simplicity of this slightest privation is rendered in its smallness and its simplicity: "That Time will come and take my love away." After all that has been said in the sonnet, this is the least of time's ruinous work and hardly an impressive display of its powers. And yet, of course, to the poet's subjectivity, it is all—the privation utter and time's power complete. If time can do this, nothing else—however objectively impressive—matters. But *can* it do this? *Is* the small, fragile, private world finally so powerless before it?

Of course, the shift to the personal world is dependent wholly on the universality of the octave and its summary in lines 9–10. The echo of "ruin" in "ruminate" (line 11) serves the poet's purpose admirably. For the ruin is *in* the rumination, is its cause and its subject, even as it forms it and forces its conclusion from it. And yet there is something continuous, repetitious, even inconclusive in "ruminate" that is also the result of "ruin." The poet cannot forget this lesson of ruin; he can never end with it; he cannot even escape from it to enjoy the present glories that precede it—only ruin itself can end his need to ruminate. In the midst of his life there is continually death. Thus the couplet:

> This thought is as a death, which cannot choose
> But weep to have that which it fears to lose.

The word "as" is actually superfluous, so fully has the very "thought" itself become the "death," the rumination become the ruin. The awareness of the dominion of "state" forces the recognition that the act of living is the act of dying —even in the highest possibilities for life that love creates. So in the last line the poet weeps not the losing, but the having, that whose loss is threatened. For it is the joy of living and of having that is transformed by the intrusion of "death" in "thought," of "ruin" in "ruminate." Thus the dominion of "state," with its ubiquitous "ruin," is total not only in its inclusion of man and nature (as in the first ten lines) but also in its embracing of the present and future as well as the past, in its forcing the present and future into the past even before they are lived.

But we know our sonneteer too well by now not to know that the deadly dominion of "state" is for him a postulate of the wormy, material world of Narcissus from which a "true love" can escape—and from which he has escaped by way of the mirror-window. We know that his rumination cannot stop with the end of Sonnet 64, that the continuing action suggested by "ruminate" suggests in its turn that he must persist in searching for a way out of the seeming consequences of unyielding, universal ruin. In 65 we find that the helpless search itself, together with the lament in poetry that accompanies it, may be the freeing agent. Still, we must grant that Sonnet 65 is at least as resentfully respectful of time's universal powers as was Sonnet 64, and as Shakespeare—in deference to his realistic sense—usually is. But out of this almost unbounded awe issues the unreasonable alternative as an almost unbelievable counter-assertion.

> Since brass, nor stone, nor earth, nor boundless sea,
> But sad mortality o'ersways their power,
> How with this rage shall beauty hold a plea,
> Whose action is no stronger than a flower?
> O, how shall summer's honey breath hold out
> Against the wrackful siege of batt'ring days,
> When rocks impregnable are not so stout,
> Nor gates of steel so strong, but Time decays?
> O fearful meditation! Where, alack,
> Shall Time's best jewel from Time's chest lie hid?
> Or what strong hand can hold his swift foot back?
> Or who his spoil of beauty can forbid?
> O, none! unless this miracle have might,
> That in black ink my love may still shine bright.

We have seen earlier that the first two lines lump together the human and natural objects of Sonnet 64 and place them equally within the domain of "mortality." The inevitable, continual, undulating conflicts within man and nature produce that "interchange of state" which justifies the use of "rage" as its universal characteristic. Universal rage against which nothing can stand—and opposed to it, out of the poet's deepest private need, the merest "plea" of "beauty." With everything levelled, with the most powerful overcome so automatically, what hope for something so delicate, "whose action is no stronger than a flower"? This is a most striking line in the force of its gentleness and of its contrast to what precedes, with "flower" reminding us—by its total opposition —of its rhyme word, "power." "Power" is the one thing the "flower" has not. But since "power" invariably fails, perhaps weakness is not necessarily a handicap, is not necessarily weak. Lines 5–6 present this opposition between vulnerable delicacy and indifferent harshness with effective phonetic enforcement: the soft, almost non-consonantal "*h*ow shall summer's *h*oney breath *h*old out" is crushed in the very saying by the cluttered "wrackful siege of batt'ring days." The remainder of the quatrain reminds us of the indelicate objects ("rocks impregnable," "gates of steel") which, in being destroyed by time, make the plight of "summer's honey breath" the more unpromising.

Now that the octave has given no slightest glimmer of an escape, the poet shows his desperation by the exclamations of line 9 and by the three successive, unsuccessful one-line questions that attempt to find a resolving metaphor (note the use of "or" to indicate the search for alternative, rapidly abandoned ways out). The first of these is the most provocative and points surely to the hopelessness of beauty's case. Beauty, after all, *is* a creation of time and exists in time: it does have a material basis, however spiritual its eventual claims. As time's creature and most precious, it is "Time's best jewel." How hide it, then, from time's all-enclosing "chest" where all that is time's and is less valuable is indifferently hoarded? Is time likely to allow the most precious to escape him when it too is rightfully his? After this closed tautology ("Time's best jewel from Time's chest"), the alternatives in the next two lines are properly unexpectant.

With only the couplet remaining, the poet seems far more pessimistic than he has been in other places where he has found more usable vehicles to exempt beauty and love from time's sway. Here he seems to have succumbed totally to the inescapable dominion of "state." The sad, absolute negation that opens the couplet acknowledges as much: "O, none!" The meek, hardly promising "unless" introduces the subjunctive possibility that is just short of impossible. From all that has been said, it should be totally impossible, and would be, except that the poet explicitly terms it a "miracle." And it is a "miracle" that would have "might," the very "power" which the seemingly powerful can never finally have and which the "flower" never tried for. May there not be a strength that arises precisely from the avoidance of it? We may recall the soft, delicate simplicity that began with Sonnet 64, line 12, and so effectively asserted its ineffectuality in lines 4 and 5 of 65. If there is no appeal against time through strength, may there—through miracle—be one through weakness? May not the weakest indeed be the strongest, the only final "power" conferred upon the "flower"?

Opposition is converted to support in just this way in the last line, when through the "might" of "miracle" the blackness that is the property of the poem's material—"ink"—becomes the agency for the constant ("still") brightness with which the poet's love shines. Here is a brilliant manipulation of the Petrarchan conceit that has the poem at once a material and a spiritual entity, the miraculous mirror-window that is a reflection of love's mirror-window. But I have now begun to put this claim in the indicative mood when it clearly belongs in the subjunctive, where Shakespeare put it. For is not its subjunctive character the essence of the miracle, and of the faith which the world's indicative truth can never affirm, even if this niggardly truth is presumptuous in denying it?

The miracle, we have observed, is descended from the

original miracle, the source of miracle, lodged in the "glassy essence" of man; in the *Sonnets* it has been seen to manifest itself in procreation, in love, in nature's cycle as a reflection of man's, and in poetry as the revelatory and incarnating art of love or discourse of love. As man begins in the mirror-window of "his glassy essence," so he ends—through an eschatological incarnation—in the final mirror-window of his all-encompassing and totally realized potentiality, in the imaged entity which is the highest man, at once the summit and the embodied summation of human history. Thus the sonnets which make the poet's most ambitious claim create the eschatology that completes his system of love's religious mythology grounded in its unique, unreasonable reason.

> When in the chronicle of wasted time
> I see descriptions of the fairest wights,
> And beauty making beautiful old rhyme
> In praise of ladies dead and lovely knights,
> Then, in the blazon of sweet beauty's best,
> Of hand, of foot, of lip, of eye, of brow,
> I see their antique pen would have express'd
> Even such a beauty as you master now.
> So all their praises are but prophecies
> Of this our time, all you prefiguring;
> And, for they look'd but with divining eyes,
> They had not skill enough your worth to sing;
>   For we, which now behold these present days,
>   Have eyes to wonder, but lack tongues to praise.

The "wasted time" in the first line suggests not only the pastness of time, time that has been spent and lost, but also—if we extend it a bit—time that has been exhausted, used up. And this notion, in view of what is to follow, opens the possibility of an end to history, now that—in the friend's existence—it has achieved its ultimate purpose. The "descriptions" in past writings were meant to refer to history's fairest creatures ("wights" lending an appropriately archaic flavor). The beauty of poetry itself was dependent on the fairness of its subjects ("beauty making beautiful old rhyme"). The poet seems to include all the "fairest wights" in his exhaustive combination of "ladies dead and lovely knights," with its complementary pair of nouns and adjectives and with the inversion of the expected groupings (lovely ladies, dead knights).

But really, we learn in the second quatrain, the descriptions do not refer to the creatures they claim to be speaking of. Rather, their individual and partial claims of beauty ("Of hand, of foot, of lip, of eye, of brow") constitute a collective attempt to express the later and totally inclusive beauty of the friend. Of course, working from their imperfect and incomplete models, the descriptions cannot fully succeed. Only the friend can "master" "such a beauty," thus in his person surpassing the "old rhyme" which could try but not quite "master" (*would* have express'd"). He thus becomes the uncomprehended objective of both all human and all poetic beauty that has preceded him. He is both the unseen model and the now realized Platonic archetype of the history of human beauty and of art.

As older "beauty" before made "beautiful old rhyme," so his beauty now makes the old rhyme less beautiful (see lines 11–12) even as it becomes the measure of the imperfect beauty that is left to old rhyme. The alliterative transformations in lines 9–10 permit the antique descriptions, meant as "*pr*aises" of their subjects, to become "*pr*ophecies" "*pr*efiguring" the poet's present friend. But, in this context, "prefiguring" is more than just another word for "prophecies." It adds a crucial precision that justifies the movement from "praises" to "prophecies." We have seen Shakespeare play on the meaning of "figure" earlier, in the "refigur'd" of Sonnet 6 (line 10). Here too we must take it literally: the descriptive praises create a fore-image of the "figure"—the form and features—of the archetype that is to be fully realized later.

It is a figure created before the figure; thus the praise indeed converts to prophecy. And in the old rhyme we find once more the mirror-window. For the subject of the antique praise is at once the actual image of the description and a preview through to the reality that stands at the end of the history of all such images and gives them their meaning. Of course, the preview must be imperfect since the final object is perfect and divination has its limitations (lines 11–12). And in the present, when the perfection exists—though as the windowed image of the past—words must fail (lines 13–14). But they are no longer needed since one need only point to it.

The key use of "prefiguring" (together with the reference to my earlier discussion of "refigur'd" in Sonnet 6) would seem once again to lead to what Auerbach has taught us of "*figura*" and the typological view of history that controls it. The "fairest wights" are clearly "figures" anticipating the "fulfillment" in the beloved friend, as Old Testament personages were seen to prefigure Christ. Thus again the movement from "praises" to "prophecies" to "prefiguring." And again, as in all the variations on the mirror-window miracle, the figures are both their historical selves and in him. As Auerbach says, "Figural interpretation establishes a connection between two events or persons in such a way that the first signifies not only itself but also the second, while the second involves or fulfills the first" (*Mimesis*, p. 64). Thus there are mirror-windows on both ends, as the phenomenal fulfillment of transcendent perfection proves to be "changeless and of all time and yet full of history" (p. 172). In the *Sonnets*, the poet can borrow this figural view for the final elevation of his friend as cosmic fulfillment, the divine-human paradox that Christian mythology lends to the enraptured discourse of love. But the "figural" is never merely figurative; it is literal, for it has its reality at both ends: "In this conception, an occurrence on earth signifies not only itself but at the same time another, which it predicts or confirms, without prejudice to the power of its concrete reality here and now. The connection between occurrences is not regarded as primarily a chronological or causal development but as a oneness within the divine plan, of which all occurrences are parts and reflections" (*Mimesis*, p. 490). The reflections that rise to share substantively in what they image create the completeness of a history that has transcended itself.

As utter fulfillment of history, the friend is closer to the second coming than to the first coming of Christ—which is why I have spoken of this movement in the *Sonnets* as eschatological. In Sonnet 106 and in those I turn to next, he is seen to stand at the absolute end of history in that he has fulfilled all the possibilities of the discrete existences that have preceded him. He transforms previous history by giving it its meaning—*his* meaning in that it has really meant him all along. In ending history he resurrects it. People from the past become images that live again as substance; praises of them become prefiguring prophecies in the transfiguring light of his final, crowning appearance on earth, after which nothing further is needed and time can have its stop. Or so, at least, the eye and mind of love must have it in creating their mythology of troth. It is no doubt true, as Auerbach says, that "in the course of the sixteenth century, the Christian-figural schema lost its hold in almost all parts of Europe" (p. 279). But here we find it reappearing most vitally, though it has been transferred—perhaps heretically, but totally and with all its implications—to the reckless claims of personal, if neo-Platonic, affection. But it took a Shakespeare to have the courage to make the secular (or is it finally secular?) transfer so bodily.[3]

The claim that the friend is the one final reality that sus-

---

[3] See my essay, "The Dark Generations of *Richard III*," *Criticism*, I (1959), especially p. 45, for an example of Shakespeare's imposition of the eschatological myth upon history even in his English Chronicle plays.

tains all the mere images of previous history is made explicitly
in Sonnet 53:

> What is your substance, whereof are you made,
> That millions of strange shadows on you tend?
> Since every one hath, every one, one shade,
> And you, but one, can every shadow lend.
> Describe Adonis, and the counterfeit
> Is poorly imitated after you.
> On Helen's cheek all art of beauty set,
> And you in Grecian tires are painted new.
> Speak of the spring, and foison of the year:
> The one doth shadow of your beauty show,
> The other as your bounty doth appear,
> And you in every blessed shape we know.
> In all external grace you have some part,
> But you like none, none you, for constant heart.

Here the terms are rather "substance" and "shadows," which
we should remember from their important role in Sonnet 37
(line 10). The opening question of Sonnet 53 expresses just
the mystery that we have seen eluding the answers of our
normal reason: what sort of substance can it be which, instead
of casting a single shadow, becomes the sole reality attended
by "millions of strange shadows"? (The singularity of all but
the friend is insisted upon in the four uses of "one" in lines
3–4.) In what follows it becomes clear that there is and has
been no other substance, that all is thrust into the friend's
shadow. Even the most beautiful creatures turn out to be not
originals but mere counterfeits of the single Platonic perfection that was to come and finally to attain worldly existence. We are back, with a certain tightening of metaphor, to
the transfigured "praises" of "ladies dead and lovely knights"
that allowed Sonnet 106 similarly to transform history into
eschatology. We should be reminded also of Sonnets 67–68,

in which the insubstantial, imitative world, with its "roses of shadow," is scornfully juxtaposed to the friend's rich and original beauty which is the sole living repository of substantive truth. Or there is Sonnet 113 ("Since I left you, mine eye is in my mind"), in which the entire phenomenal world is transformed for the poet through the intervening presence of the friend which "shapes" that world to himself. Here in Sonnet 113 is an epistemological analogue of the historical process of miracle the other sonnets have been urging: in Sonnet 113 the friend affects what phenomenal reality can be for the eyes of love, as in the others he affects historical reality in the same way. In all of them the friend, as mirror-window, is—like the Christian Trinity—at once one and many: as substantive entity he is seen as the unique substance that absorbs all entities and reduces the others to shadows of himself. Consequently, the myriads of history and of the phenomenal world are reduced to images struggling in their individual incompleteness to achieve their reality in him. In Sonnet 53 the friend's unitary truth absorbs the natural world as well as the historical process. Springtime and harvest are also reflections of him, so that the poet, in lines 12 and 13, can make his most extravagant claim for this single incarnation of the numberless manifestations of beauty ("And you in every blessed shape we know. / In all external grace you have some part").[4]

Finally, of course, the mythology proclaimed by love's mystic can take its meaning only in its relations to the cold-blooded world. At his best, as we have repeatedly seen, Shakespeare is most aware of the stubborn persistence of niggardly marketplace facts that demand recognition even by him who would transcend them. His most satisfying attempts to pro-

[4] Unfortunately, there is a serious falling off in the final line of the poem, where, neglecting the terms of the sonnet in favor of the common Petrarchan piety, the poet expresses the greater superiority of his friend in the unique possession of internal grace ("constant heart").

duce the poetry that is love's self-justifying discourse are those
—like Sonnet 74 or 87 among many I might mention—that
arise out of, and remain responsive to, the common world's
apparent truths. It is this extraordinary juxtaposing of the
most factual and most supernal—or rather the rendering of
the second by means of the first—that makes the unit com-
prised of Sonnets 30 and 31 among the most rewarding in
the sequence.

When to the sessions of sweet silent thought
I summon up remembrance of things past,
I sigh the lack of many a thing I sought
And with old woes new wail my dear time's waste.
Then can I drown an eye (unus'd to flow)
For precious friends hid in death's dateless night,
And weep afresh love's long since cancell'd woe,
And moan th' expense of many a vanish'd sight.
Then can I grieve at grievances foregone,
And heavily from woe to woe tell o'er
The sad account of fore-bemoaned moan,
Which I new pay as if not paid before.
    But if the while I think on thee, dear friend,
    All losses are restor'd and sorrows end.

Thy bosom is endeared with all hearts
Which I by lacking have supposed dead;
And there reigns love, and all love's loving parts,
And all those friends which I thought buried.
How many a holy and obsequious tear
Hath dear religious love stol'n from mine eye,
As interest of the dead, which now appear
But things remov'd that hidden in thee lie!
Thou art the grave where buried love doth live,
Hung with the trophies of my lovers gone,
Who all their parts of me to thee did give:
That due of many now is thine alone.

Their images I lov'd I view in thee,
And thou—all they—hast all the all of me.

In Sonnet 30 the poet indulges in just the sort of mourning that we saw him asking his friend—if somewhat ironically—to reject coldly in Sonnet 71 ("No longer mourn for me"). There are other relations between Sonnets 30 and 71, especially in the tone of the two sonnets with their opposition between sentiment and marketplace. Indeed, perhaps it is the futility of marketplace methods in Sonnet 30 to appreciate the powers and needs of affections that leads in Sonnet 71 to the somewhat self-pitying indictment of the "vile world" in its emotional unresponsiveness.

Shakespeare's strategy in Sonnet 30 of using the language of law and bookkeeping should by now be familiar to us. His joining in metaphor the world of sentiment and of the marketplace has been effective in many of the sonnets (I need mention only Sonnets 4, 74, and 87). Such bits of soft sentiment as "sweet silent thought," sighs, wails, drowning eyes, grievings and moans, are held in the businesslike framework of "sessions" to which one is harshly summoned up, of woes that are "cancell'd," of "expense," accounts, and payments. We must be puzzled by a phrase like "precious friends," which can be read into either world, or both; or by the telling over the "sad account," which can refer to the narrating of his sentimental tale or to the "telling" activity of the auditor. But it is just this language which has a foot in both worlds that seems to prove how thoroughly the poet has proved their union. And yet this union should be a shocking one, a yoking of elements that are indeed most heterogeneous. What business can these disparate areas of human experience have with each other, especially in these sonnets which have emphasized the polar conflict between matter, in all its niggardliness, and the open generosity of spirit?

It is precisely the poet's error that he tries to submit his woes to the auditor's assumptions and operations. He is so subdued by common-sense worldliness that he feels forced to render the intangible as tangible, the immeasurable sorrows as measurable items. At the same time, he undercuts his sentimental insistences, presented too howlingly in the most obvious and unimaginative terms of lamentation (four uses of "woe," three of "moan," alliterative emphasis on "woes," "wail," and "waste," among the many obvious devices), by enclosing them within the matter-of-factness of marketplace reduction.[5] The dominant frustration in the poem is the poet's inability to make this reduction work, as the world of lamentation resists being converted into items in a ledger. Distressed by the endlessly resistant ineffability of lamentation, the poet still seeks to be an auditor of the affections and discovers in the sonnet how unsuccessful this procedure is fated to be. He treats his various mournings as items to be entered in the account book (especially lines 7–12), but the things persist in refusing to act accordingly: the woes, grievances, and moans will not permit themselves to be balanced. They never cease their demands for further payment. Endlessly costly, they cannot be isolated, made into finite entities that have an end. The auditor-poet thinks he has paid them off, only to have them still unremoved on the debit side. That he must ever "new wail" "old woes," ever spending his sorrow anew, leaves him at the end of his arithmetical tether. The "woe" is "long since cancell'd" and thus ought to be done with; but there it is, still agonizingly there, demanding to be wept "afresh." It is this persistence of sorrow that makes the repetitions in each line of the third quatrain so effective ("grieve at grievances," "woe to woe," "fore-bemoaned moan," "pay as if not paid"). The sorrow will continue to be

[5] Of course, the poet-persona's error and weakness of vision are not to be transferred to Shakespeare, who so carefully exposes them to us, forces them to fail in Sonnet 30, and—with the poet-persona—corrects them in Sonnet 31, after the dialectical process has done its work.

181

repeated again and again—grievances to be regrieved, the account of woes to be told over and over as the moans are to be always bemoaned. For lamentation is turned into a most unsuccessful business enterprise that must pay and pay for what has been many times paid for. The repetition shifts from the commonplace emotional terms in lines 9–11 (grieve, woe, moan) to that most central marketplace term, "pay," in line 12. The latter reveals the framework in which the others have been considered all along—and suggests why this consideration has been inadequate to the needs of the poet in his lament. Affection cannot be reduced to ledger entries; what can take care of items in an account is inapplicable to the immeasurable world that is beyond cancelling. Perhaps we should think of that star in Sonnet 116, "Whose worth's unknown, although his highth be taken." For once again we are faced with truth's inaccessibility to troth.

The couplet reveals how thoroughly—and futilely—the poet has exhausted his marketplace methods, which have at once lent specificity to his lament and revealed their own bankruptcy. After all the payments and repayments which leave the pain still there and unalleviated, suddenly there is the cavalier gesture of the couplet and an unearned leap to total release:

> But if the while I think on thee, dear friend,
> All losses are restor'd and sorrows end.

All reasonable ways out having failed, the poet turns to the present friend, and the endlessly troublesome troubles are at an end. The "sessions of sweet silent thought" are adjourned for him to "think on" his dear friend. The attempt to make legal and financial sense of his thought is abandoned for the sheer, unreasoning immediacy of love. Affection's past laments can be resolved not by submitting them to the consolations of normal reason but by transforming them into affection's present joys. With the mere thought of the friend, then, the bottomless pit of payment no longer yawns. The finality of the reversal in the poem's last word is total: sorrows are at once at an absolute "end." Further, not only is there no need to pay further, but all that has been paid is "restor'd." Of course, the double action of "losses" is like that of other words in the poem that reach at once toward the financial and the sentimental poles: the "losses" are also the human losses, those "precious friends hid in death's dateless night" for whom he has so endlessly mourned. For, as Sonnet 31 insists, the poet has lost no one.

The shift from the futility of the auditor's care in the first twelve lines to the success of the lover's reckless leap in the couplet—the sudden replacement of affection by affection instead of the sensible replacement of affection by measurement—these leave us at the end of Sonnet 30 perhaps unconvinced, but persuaded of what the ardor of love can lead the lover to insist upon, and to deny, in his transcendence of the world. But the poetic entity is not yet complete, since its second half in Sonnet 31 is undertaken in order to earn metaphorically the rash extravagance of the couplet of Sonnet 30, its total restoration of "*all* losses" and its "end" to endless sorrows. The dead he has mourned are literally resurrected—indeed reincarnated—in the collective and yet uniquely singular entity of the beloved friend, who becomes their magical mirror-window. They were only "supposed dead." The poet suggests that he was misled by his missing their appearance into making this supposition: that he was deluded by his trust in flesh into seeing it as the sole form of living and was unprepared for the flowing together of "distincts." Thus they were wrongly "thought buried" (line 4). But later in the sonnet, as his metaphor develops, we find them "buried" after all (line 9)—buried in the friend, of course, and there living still—though as "things remov'd," "hidden" in him (line 8) rather than in "death's dateless night" (Sonnet 30, line 6).

If "hidden," then "buried"; but as "buried *love*" in him it can *live*. How different this burial is from that supposed burial which led to the mourning of Sonnet 30, and how different this "grave," this tomb which is the womb of further and more complete life ("Thou art the grave where buried love doth live").

In this sonnet the poet can afford to look back upon the "supposed" burial and the mistaken mourning it caused. After acknowledging in the first quatrain his supposition as a worldling, he speaks of the tears that love has stolen from his eye. He is in effect referring to his endless lamentation in the first twelve lines of Sonnet 30, except that he now sees these tears as being unjustly stolen rather than as being justly collected, since his trothful vision is leading him to see the burial of his friends as a form of rebirth, an occasion that merits joy rather than sorrow. The tears were taken before "as interest of the dead"—that is, on behalf of the (seeming) dead and their just claim upon his affections. But there has been too much financial terminology in Sonnet 30 for us to ignore the other sense of "interest"—especially when it has been used in just the bank-clerk's sense of increment with respect to the dead in Sonnet 74 ("My life hath in this line some interest," line 3). Thus "interest" must also refer to what is left over as surplus and memorial. As we have seen in Sonnet 30, tears are the sole possible survivors, the sole proper "interest" of the materialistic version of death. With the end of matter in death and his worms, the auditor's mentality must demand something tangible, material, as *its* surviving "interest" (and we know how the very poem itself, the "this," functioned to elevate and even spiritualize this demand in Sonnet 74). The only material "interest of the dead," so long as they are seen as merely dead, is "many a holy and obsequious tear," referred to in Sonnet 31 after having been dwelled upon in Sonnet 30. But if love suspends the material sense of "property," it gives rise to the magical "interest" of the new entity, the beloved friend, who is the corporate resurrection of all the old entities. That other financial term, "due" ("That due of many now is thine alone"), indicates what happens to "interest" in the new irrational consideration: the friend, as the miraculous "grave" that allows "buried love" to "live," now has as his "due" or "interest" not the sad matter of tears (which were both inadequate and, it turned out, uncalled for) but the just inheritance of all the affection that love has stored through his predecessors who have become himself. The final line insists that the identity, the incarnation, be seen as complete, with no one and nothing held back: "And thou —*all* they—hast *all* the *all* of me." The unqualified "all" has been prepared for from the final line of Sonnet 30 ("*All* losses are restor'd and sorrows end"), through Sonnet 31, lines 1 ("*all* hearts"), 3 ("*all* love's loving parts"), and 4 ("*all* those friends"), to the climactic line 11 ("Who *all* their parts of me to thee did give"). No wonder the friend now is nothing less than *all* of them and has nothing less than *all* of the poet. The poet sees that selfhood has merged with thou-ness and them-ness. In this marriage of *all* true minds, the distinctness of subject and object, and the distinctness of persons past and the person present have been obliterated into a present union that is total and transcendent in its sovereign invulnerability to the "impediments" of "state." The union is consummate in the identities that are lost in it even as they achieve their fulfillment—their reborn and still living incarnation—in it.

Nowhere does Shakespeare more ambitiously and explicitly lay claim to the miracle that approaches eschatology through incarnation, coming at them out of the "common things" of the marketplace in all their precious distinctness. The couplet of Sonnet 30, with its seemingly sentimental leap out of the common-sense hopelessness that precedes it, comes to be justified by the poet's creating his beloved friend, in Sonnet 31, as the total and crowning summation of individuated histories, which have now retreated into mere "images" (Sonnet 31, line 13). But these images do not "die single," as does that of the Narcissus of Sonnet 3, since they die to a new life through love, becoming a constitutive part of the friend as the total reality that lives now as the corporate past. Of course, compared to the rhapsodic historic sweep of sonnets like 106 and 53, Sonnets 30–31 would appear to urge a more modest and personal eschatology: the end and transcendence of the poet's private emotional history. Still for his subjectivity and its troth, this history is enough, for it is total. This history has been the cosmos of the entire sonnet sequence; and only the magical discourse of poetry—and of these poems—could create the cosmology that both permits and resolves the mysteries of a substance that flows among its shifting entities. The discreteness of their images that "die single" (Sonnet 3, line 14) is dissolved into unions that defy the more common reason of our world.

We may freely admit that Sonnet 31, as microcosm of the workings of the entire sequence, finally only "rationalizes" the hasty miracle of Sonnet 30 into the special terms of the unreasonable reason of the system—which is to say that it converts the mere claim to miracle into substantive metaphor. It turns the claim into a mirror-window by making a mirror-window of the friend. In this sense, we may say that Sonnet 31 earns the claim of the couplet of Sonnet 30 rather than proves it. For the mode of discourse of a poem as a mirror-window must, like the metaphor at its root, only earn and never try to prove lest it convert itself into another mode of discourse. So Sonnet 31 gives us the miracle still, though now in an embodiment analogous to the Christian Trinity, and keeps it unreduced and unreducible—as unreducible as metaphor. This is the discourse of love's mystic, using the reason of love's unreason. As such, these sonnets are discursive testimony of how love's unreason must work: they represent the way love's unreason speaks. They become both act and repository of faith.

But here poetics must enter, as we have seen it enter each time Shakespeare has offered the very existence of his sonnet, itself a miraculous mirror-window of the word and spirit made body, as evidence of the mirror-window of love. For Shakespeare the problem of unity and duality in love and in the metaphors of religion is one with the problem of unity and duality—of mirror and window—in the language of poetry. As he solves one problem, he solves the other. This is the justification of the union I force in this book between Shakespeare's *Sonnets* and literary theory.

John Crowe Ransom long sought to tie poetry to love through the opposition between what he termed "structure" and "texture," an opposition that for him arose from and yielded the "precious object." Except in poetry and love, for Ransom as for the Shakespeare of the *Sonnets,* the modern practical world values objects only insofar as it can use them. For this world, the mere labelling of life's furniture is enough to ensure its functioning for us. The poet, like the chaste lover, can value the object he perceives for its own sake with an attention that is in excess of its utility value and irrelevant to it. He must have nothing less than the total object (in effect, the object as subject) since he chooses to cherish rather than to use it. So normal discourse, with its exclusive interest in "structure," a marshalled and totalitarian discourse, can give way to the brilliant wastefulness of poetry, in which there is a "texture" that represents our devotion to the object and that exceeds the demands of structure, is irrelevant to these demands, even as pure affection exceeds and is irrelevant to the interestedness of use.[6] As reward in Platonic

---

[6] See *The New Apologists for Poetry* (Minneapolis, 1956), especially pp. 82–87, for a more detailed discussion of Ransom's position for

love, Shakespeare claims the incarnation that is substantive. Similarly, in poetry Ransom claims that the wastefulness can allow discovery of a body in the word, that the wayward texture can allow the poem to take on its own life, with all the magic of a primitive effigy, as the word itself becomes the object of our devotion. Critics can stop merely "using" poems, as poems can have us stop merely "using" objects and words —in the same way as the existentialist in both Shakespeare and Ransom would have us stop using "persons" (subjects) lest we reduce them to usable "things" (objects). And we may properly be reminded of Shakespeare's dwelling, in Sonnets 4 and 9, on the perversely inhuman "use" which is "abuse."

So long as we refuse to stop with the word's transparent function as window, we can be allowed to find in it a set of closed mirrors, a universe of words as things. But as reward for our attention, we may share Alice's blessing and find the mirror opening outward again to a new world, so much like our old one, and yet after all new in our perceptive capacity to grasp it, although, like that other wonderland, it may seem like nonsense to our normal logical processes, whose inadequacy it is bent on revealing. If we proceed this way, we are retracing Shakespeare's way. Shakespeare inherited from his tradition the immense capacities for manipulation of the mirror-window image. We have seen from the outset the extent to which he submitted himself to the conventions he was transcending. May we not find in his final respect for these conventions, tempered occasionally by an almost supercilious tolerance for their extravagance, an embracing of the absurd in them that is his poetic equivalent for the chivalric fidelity to an archaic troth that is the very heart of these son-

its own sake. It should be mentioned incidentally that there is considerable irony in finding a sanction for Ransom's approach in Shakespeare's *Sonnets*. For Ransom treated these sonnets quite scornfully when he turned his critical attention to them. See "Shakespeare at Sonnets," *The World's Body* (New York, 1938), pp. 270–303.

nets? This is his testament of faith as poet that accompanies his testament of faith as lover. He can get to his spiritual claims of a union that is at once neo-Platonic, Petrarchan, and Courtly through accepting the convention that leads him to reject the terms of the material, contingent world—the world whose "realistic" demands he has tried to satisfy by distrusting the convention enough to introduce at full strength the marketplace reductions of the convention. But troth claims the final allegiance and transcendence in poetry as in love, perhaps again testifying to their ultimate oneness. Thus Sonnet 76, in which the poet's dedication to the conventional applies at once to method and substance, to poetics and thematics:[7]

> Why is my verse so barren of new pride?
> So far from variation or quick change?
> Why, with the time, do I not glance aside
> To new-found methods and to compounds strange?
> Why write I still all one, ever the same,
> And keep invention in a noted weed,
> That every word doth almost tell my name,
> Showing their birth, and where they did proceed?
> O, know, sweet love, I always write of you,
> And you and love are still my argument:
> So all my best is dressing old words new,
> Spending again what is already spent;
>   For as the sun is daily new and old,
>   So is my love still telling what is told.

Through his "invention in a noted weed," his inimitable signature and unique—if traditional—argument carried in "every word," Shakespeare forced his poetry (the "this" which is both act and repository), by the very mode of its be-

[7] I must record here my debt to a student of many years back, Miss Grace Billings, whose sensitive reading of this sonnet first made me aware of the full breadth of its applicability.

ing, to earn his right to claim his special meaning for it, to become the source as well as the mouth of that meaning. In using the body of religious mythology to symbolize the creation of love's faith, its troth, Shakespeare has created a substantive or "corporeal" poetry that is the discursive equivalent of that troth. The critical theory with which I began and to which I now turn again is merely following his lead. Shakespeare has made this poetry, in its union with its mythology, the *in* and the *through*, the mirror-window of discourse, that by theoretical extension creates the profoundest possibilities and prospects for poetry generally, as the finest art.

III

THE POWER OF POETIC

EFFIGY

THE POWER OF POETIC
EFFIGY

WE HAVE SEEN the body of Shakespeare's *Sonnets* at once as mirror and—through remaining mirror—as enchanted window. That is to say, we have seen it as the source of the very meaning of which it is the mouth, as the repository of the faith which in its writing it enacts—in summary, as the memorial tomb of the love to which, as womb, it gives everlasting life. We can recall here the poem as the entombing and resurrecting urn of *The Canonization:*

> We'll build in sonnets pretty rooms;
> As well a well-wrought urn becomes
> The greatest ashes, as half-acre tombs,
> And by these hymns, all shall approve
> Us canonized for love ...

and of *The Phoenix and Turtle:*

> To this urn let those repair
> That are either true or fair;
> For these dead birds sigh a prayer.[1]

As the discourse of love's reason, whose argument is constituted by the very method of argument, it is the ritual gesture and offering to love, whose content is in its form.

This union returns us to Philip Wheelwright and his use of the "Law of Participation" that relates art to primitive ritual in its monistic claim of substantive oneness between referent and sign. The referent "participates" in the sign, achieves identity in the sign as it converts the sign to substance. This monistic claim characterizes the primitive sense

---

[1] It is to both these passages in their multiple meanings that Cleanth Brooks similarly refers in justifying the title and method of *The Well Wrought Urn* (New York, 1947). See especially p. 19.

of language which we have observed in Wheelwright, the sense that finds the rain literally *in* the smoke that the Navaho uses to bring it forth, the sense that we saw Frazer observe in those tribes who eat their gods. It is, of course, the same immediacy of primitive religious experience which destroys for the participant any distinction between the wafer and the body or between the wine and the blood of Christ. As in Frazer, the substance of the god literally enters the mere symbol for him, and the effigy breathes life.

But this is a way of language no longer available to a sophisticated culture. The spontaneity of a language that could once take immediacy for granted is dissolved into a more conceptual, "Platonized" language, so that immediacy must be worked for. (I use the notion of the Platonic here in the spirit of Ransom, Tate, and Wimsatt and Brooks, as I described it at the start of this book. I mean it to refer to that mythical stage in the conceptual development of culture when the separation between words and world, between ideas and phenomenal reality, becomes absolute and unbridgeable. As it becomes intellectualized, the culture loses its naiveté and becomes sophisticated. Thus I use Plato representatively rather than historically, just as these other critics do: every culture has its Platos to bring its language to the fallen state, and ours undoubtedly had many of them long before the historical Plato.[2]) The monistic experience itself doubtlessly

---

[2] In his appeal to "miraculism" which I traced at the very start, Ransom rather uses Hobbes "the naturalist" (meaning by this term "a person who studies nature not because he loves it but because he wants to use it, approaches it from the standpoint of common sense, and sees it thin and not thick") as the dully civilized defender of the dualistic principle of language. He quotes Hobbes: "The second cause of absurd assertions I ascribe to the giving of names of 'bodies' to 'accidents,' or of 'accidents' to 'bodies,' as they do that say 'faith is infused' or 'inspired,' when nothing can be 'poured' or 'breathed' into anything but body. . . ." The judgment and the scorn are unquestionable. ("Poetry: a Note in Ontology," *The World's Body*, especially pp. 135–140.) I should add that, since writers like Rosemund Tuve and Father

still occurs as pre-linguistic experience, but it is lost to the "Platonized" development of language as tool, of language as rationally distinguishable from the world to which it means to refer. Indeed, as we have seen earlier, my complaint against Wheelwright's claims for "expressive truth" was grounded largely on his equation of the ways in which the language of poetry, myth, ritual, and religion functioned, and on his consequent failure to distinguish adequately between the subjective medium of faith and the objective medium of discourse. For I see a special character in poetry that arises out of a difference in its mode of discourse; but myth, ritual, and religion rather depend on a difference in the mode of experience—on faith rather than discourse— although in a sophisticated culture this difference is not reflected in any uniqueness of discourse.

How can a sophisticated culture manage the monistic way of language that was lost to it in its early days? If we assume our continuing need for the totally substantive, fully empowered effigy, our need to feel an immediacy in the word that can match the immediacy of our experience, in short our need to transcend the empty character of words as pointing tools, how can our Platonized language in its fallen dualism permit the need to be satisfied? Obviously I am trying to say that poetry can still be this effigy for a culture that has lost all its less self-conscious ways of achieving it.

I have shown at length, in dealing with the contextual nature of the poem, that like effigy it does seem to begin

---

Walter J. Ong, it is Ramism that is often seen as the divisive instrument for modern Western culture, forging an ineluctable word-thing dichotomy for the sake of a purer logic and a freer science. For a most exciting transformation of this aspect of Ramism into an attitude that permits the "corporealizing" of language, see Jackson I. Cope, *The Metaphoric Structure of* PARADISE LOST (Baltimore, 1962), especially pp. 27–49, 177–179. This book, published after my own manuscript was completed, seems to me, in its theoretical contribution to poetics, similar to my own and a corroboration of it.

in imitation, using what seem to be extramurally directed signs. Yet we have seen imitation as enemy to a poetry going it on its own. I earlier tried to reduce any theory to "imitationism" that ended by making the work responsible to an extramural "object of imitation," whether that "object" was an archetypal structure, a complex of historical-cultural forces, or a private, imaginative vision, so long as it was a formulated entity pre-existing the poem that was to translate (and, thus, to "imitate") it. Aristotle was right in saying that imitation pleases and that much of our pleasure in art consists in its imitation; but he was wrong in saying that imitation, or the pleasure it arouses, is the end of art. Imitation is no more the end of art than pleasure is, and the reasons are the same in both cases. For imitation is only the beginning of art: it is, as my allegory of the glass house was intended to show, the lure, the deceptive promise of pleasure through mere recognition. But we engage this mild pleasure at our peril. Its consequences can be revolutionary when we discover the substantive god within as the effigy takes on its magic.

This notion of effigy seems just what I need, although like "icon" or other such terms in recent use it too seems open to the charge of "imitationism."[3] Like the icon or idol, the effigy is after all but a copy and thus also seems to point outside, to keep us within the duality of language, to act as mere window. Still it seems right somehow, in that more than other terms it carries forth the notion of the immanent god. By recognizing that in primitive magic and religion the effigy could bear the immanent reality substantively within what from the sophisticated modern view *seems* but a copy, I can recognize also the similar indwelling god within a contextual poetry and see this poetry as a self-conscious equiv-

<hr/>

[3] For a most effective reduction of the theory of the "iconic sign" to the doctrine of imitation, see Eliseo Vivas, "Aesthetics and the Theory of Signs," *Creation and Discovery* (New York, 1955), pp. 249–265, especially pp. 256, 264–265.

alent of the effigy. For to construct the effigy—or the poem —is by craft to reduce that uncontrollable and alien outside force to the manageable dimensions of human vision and human control, to give it a destiny that answers the desires of the crafty creator of the externalized and shrunken replica. The effigy is created out of the need both to control and to worship: it is created out of both reverential awe and reverential love—an awe that is aware of the complex unmanageability and even unintelligibility of its "object" in any more unstylized and uncrafted a form, an awe that is the expression of the primitive man's love for his ruthless, undiscriminating gods or the poet's love for the bewildering complex of powers that beset him from within and without. It is an awe and a love that create the god, or the enemy-asgod, to destroy him, to destroy his humanly confusing, confounding power through creating him, through reducing him to the dimensions of the world ruled by the mastery of human craft. Thus the threatening chaos is destroyed—or overcome— through the imposition of human order, in a way similar to that we have seen in Mann's *Doctor Faustus,* where giving despair "a voice," giving the creature a voice for its woe, becomes the highest form of conquest. This subduing of the threatening chaos to human order is the role of the poet as it is the role of the primitive magician and worshipper,[4] and as such reveals that what we say of the primitive and his effigy can be as true—and more self-consciously true—of the poet and his creation.

The monistic power of effigy depends, of course, on the

[4] Wheelwright properly questions Frazer's emphasis on magic control as the originating principle of primitive ritual. Wheelwright sees this emphasis as a product of Frazer's anti-religious positivism and sees it as leading to the neglect of the very important element of pure worship in ritual (*The Burning Fountain,* pp. 175–179). One must surely grant the presence of both elements, although I hardly see them as being opposed to one another. To seek to subdue and control what one loves and fears can be an essential part of an expression of that love and fear.

union in the symbolic experience that responds to it. In the language of primitive ritual, the source of this power was located in what Lévy-Bruhl thought of as the "pre-logical" psychology, the pre-scientific belief of him whom the effigy served. The efficacy with which it functioned as monistic symbol did not necessarily depend on characteristics of the image itself, on the skill that produced the likeness, but on the power of the animistic faith that allowed the "Law of Participation" to operate. In the case of bread and wine, transubstantiation could take place without any dependence at all on the form of the object, provided it had certain minimal and quite arbitrary properties. The god enters the object by the mere fiat of the primitive imagination acting within the religious mythology that allowed *its* naive version of science. We can recall the impatience of that self-confident 19th century positivist, Frazer, as he characterized primitive magic as "a false science as well as an abortive art" (*The Golden Bough*, p. 11). For the primitive imagination needed no more. Indeed, no one can serve better than Frazer as our example of the more sophisticated stage of culture, whose language—key to his epistemology—has been Platonized to the point where it can no longer comprehend the monistic experience of the symbol. This experience must now seem as shamefully obsolete as the primitive language of "participation" that uttered it. It must seem like utter nonsense and an affront to civilized man's common-sense reason, which springs from the concept of language as tool, as empty sign to be ruthlessly used in the service of things in a universe controlled by a simple epistemological realism. Despite our complacent feeling that, in our understanding of the religious experience in the last half century, we have come beyond Frazer's reductions, must we not admit, however uncomfortably, that there is an extent to which he speaks for all of us in our unguarded moments of sophisticated skepticism, when he expresses his own blindness, so representative of civilized reason confronted by the immediacy of primitive language?

"It is now easy to understand why a savage should desire to partake of the flesh of an animal or man whom he regards as divine. By eating the body of the god he shares in the god's attributes and powers. And when the god is a corn-god, the corn is his proper body; when he is a vine-god, the juice of the grape is his blood; and so by eating the bread and drinking the wine the worshipper partakes of the real body and blood of his god. Thus the drinking of wine in the rites of a vine-god like Dionysus is not an act of revelry, it is a solemn sacrament. Yet a time comes when reasonable men find it hard to understand how any one in his senses can suppose that by eating bread or drinking wine he consumes the body or blood of a deity. 'When we call corn Ceres and wine Bacchus,' says Cicero, 'we use a common figure of speech; but do you imagine that anybody is so insane as to believe that the thing he feeds upon is a god?' "[5]

Here is just the necessary claim of a reasonable culture: let us always keep the figurative only figurative and never confuse it with the literal by suggesting it might be substantive. How fitting that Cicero be cited as our representative rationalist who, in making too sensible a philosophy of language, reduces the elusiveness of poetry to the sound management of rhetoric.[6]

[5] *The Golden Bough*, pp. 498–499.

[6] Auerbach has a similar view of the incapacity of the Roman "mentality" and language to grasp the sort of union that defies the distinctness governed by temporality and causality. He, of course, is speaking of the double reality of the *"figura"*:

". . . if an occurrence like the sacrifice of Isaac is interpreted as prefiguring the sacrifice of Christ, so that in the former the latter is as it were announced and promised, and the latter 'fulfills' (the technical term is *figuram implere*) the former, then a connection is established between two events which are linked neither temporally nor causally—a connection which it is impossible to establish by reason in the horizontal dimension (if I may be permitted to use this term for a temporal exten-

III. THE POWER OF POETIC EFFIGY

Of course, we have seen from the start of this essay that recent apologists for poetry have preferred to embrace the miraculous power of poetry to produce the substantive transfer. Spitzer was one of those who related this power to religious mystery. We have seen him dwell on transubstantiation in words that are powerfully relevant to what we have seen in Frazer and Wheelwright. Thus, speaking of Marvell's "Nymph Complaining for the Death of Her Fawn," Spitzer can say: "The fawn who lies in a bed of lilies and feeds on roses (that is, is pure as the lily and embodies, like the rose, the flame of love) may become lilies and roses because organic beings may, in a sort of mythological metabolism, become what they eat."[7] Still, however related to "medieval religious beliefs," this remains "a miracle of the poet's making" and can be no more than "quasi-religious." In the reasonable world only the poet can work to make it.

It is surely more difficult to get the god inside his imaged likeness once language has lost its monistic sense of "participation" to the Platonic dualism between referent and sign. The god must now be forced inside by the self-conscious manipulation of language that turns itself into a special containing and empowering agent. I have said that the monistic

---

sion). . . . The horizontal, that is the temporal and causal, connection of occurrences is dissolved; the here and now is no longer a mere link in an earthly chain of events, it is simultaneously something which has always been, and which will be fulfilled in the future; and strictly, in the eyes of God, it is something eternal, something omni-temporal, something already consummated in the realm of fragmentary earthly event. This conception of history is magnificent in its homogeneity, but it was completely alien to the mentality of classical antiquity, it annihilated that mentality down to the very structure of its language, at least of its literary language, which—with all its ingenious and nicely shaded conjunctions, its wealth of devices for syntactic arrangement, its carefully elaborated system of tenses—became wholly superfluous as soon as earthly relations of place, time, and cause had ceased to matter, as soon as a vertical connection, ascending from all that happens, converging in God, alone became significant." (*Mimesis*, pp. 73–74)

[7] *Essays on English and American Literature*, pp. 108–109.

power of effigy depends on the union in the symbolic experience that responds to it, and that it was the fiat of "prelogical" psychology and "pre-logical" sense of language rather than the qualities of the object that allowed this experience to the primitive. The authentication of his naive language was thus self-induced and sustained by his animistic faith. However, any possibility of this kind of symbolic experience must be externally and objectively authenticated once our sophisticated sense of language and the epistemology it sanctions have taken hold. In our late language only the object can force this experience upon us, closing its context to enclose its god and make us respond to a monistic sense of "presence" in the symbol. This sense now can arise only in response to the object that cuts off our normal, Platonized language response. Hence the obsession of modern critics with the linguistic miracle of incarnation, the use in recent aesthetics of terms like "presentational symbol" or "iconic sign," and the rewarding efforts, in practical criticism, of writers like Burckhardt to show how a poem must "drive a wedge between words and their meanings . . . and thereby inhibit our all too ready flight from them to the things they point to" in order to give "the word as entity primacy over the word as sign."

This discussion may throw new light on Shakespeare's double strategy in the *Sonnets*. He appeals continually to the "participation" analogies that his traditional Christianity makes available to him in its assertions of substantive transfer in the Trinity and the Sacrament and in its typological reading of history. But he cannot allow these to stand as mere assertions based on the fiat of faith. For he is dealing with poetry, which must as discourse create its own objective sanction, and not with direct religious experience, for which the immediacy of faith is sanction enough. Though he is to make the poetry—as source and mouth of meaning, as ritual gesture of love—force a response that has the immediacy and the symbolic union of the religious response, he must do it, as we have seen, not just by proclaiming equations between the unions asserted in dogma and those he asserts for love, but by using these analogous unions as the materials for a poetry that *earns* its way to its own union within the self-enclosed walls of meaning that poetic devices have tightly constructed. For a poem to use borrowed materials that claim the mirror-window miracle is not enough; it must be its own mirror-window to make the claim good aesthetically. That is to say, it is not enough to see a literary work typologically, in the manner of Northrop Frye, to see it as part of a universal allegory, as borrowing or translating elements which are part of the grand mythic scheme that enters and controls all literature. Rather, the work must make its way to its own totality of system, so that if it uses typological materials, it creates them anew, always earning afresh its right to use them.

If, then, the poem as both offering and repository is both the speech and the act of love's unreasonable reason, it is because as speech, as discourse, it has become a self-conscious, highly wrought replica that forces us to see what the symbolic immediacy of the religious response can be, how it can come to mean. So Shakespeare has it both ways, appealing to the immediacy sanctioned by naive faith and to the immediacy sanctioned by the self-conscious operations of sophisticated discourse. That is, he appropriates by analogy those Christian assertions of "participation" (in the Trinity, the Sacrament, and Biblical typology) which serve him as what I have earlier termed "signs," and he converts them into elements of a thoroughly symbolic system that enforces its own substantive oneness, thereby earning aesthetically as symbols the pre-aesthetic, substantive claims of the borrowed Christian signs. As the materials of faith, the latter may very well be "un-earned" in discourse, but when they enter as the materials for poetry, they must—like all materials for poetry, as they are materials *before* poetry—undergo the transformation required to make them part of an earned symbolic system that has body, that is its own entity.

I have more than once (see especially my discussion of Sonnets 30–31) acknowledged that earning is not proving, and that the poem ought not to prove even as it *can* not prove. For it does not assert, following Sir Philip Sidney's dictum: "the Poet . . . nothing affirmes, and therefore never lyeth." Shakespeare, for example, is not asserting the philosophical truth of love's reason. He is not making propositional claims about the Christ-like nature and Christ-like role of his friend; but neither is he merely flattering him ingeniously and extravagantly, in accordance with an insincere convention that calls for extravagant ingenuity. Instead, Shakespeare presents us with a true lover, a total devotee of love, as his poet-persona; and the poems are created out of the vision of his fidelity. This trothful version of reality, which is the only version it can countenance, creates its mythology of the beloved as its Christ, the end of its history. Its world can have nothing less. Its vision is to be aesthetically earned by the substantive union that makes it body, by the existence of this poem. And if it does not prove its vision, it can only scorn the knowledge given by those assertions that aim to prove. For proof leads to the claim of truth, whose niggardliness the troth of faith's mythology sees as worm-ridden. Shakespeare's task is to convert the rapturous equations of love's mystic into a total presentative body of language, to convert claims *about* a mirror-window miracle into the presentative immediacy of a form of which the mirror-window is the controlling feature open to our aesthetic perception. Thus Spitzer's three criteria—poetic vision, historic greatness, and organic artistry —can be united in the aesthetic moment.

The Christian still capable of undergoing the "participation" experience may not need this kind of discursive manipulation of it; but without it he is undergoing unauthenticated

III. THE POWER OF POETIC EFFIGY

religious experience that has its own arbitrary sanction but is not to be confused—as I think it is confused by Wheelwright —with the aesthetic experience fostered upon believer or nonbeliever by the contextual order of poetry. For, outside the realm of a wholly contextual art such as I described at length earlier in this book, the unified symbolic experience is no longer available in our normal language, and there is no longer any sense of what language can be or do that could make it available. The effigy available in the realm of faith is no longer accessible to the realm of language except within the distortions required to produce this wholly contextual art. Again, unlike Wheelwright, we must not confuse that monistic immediacy the impulse to which and the sanction for which are from inside, from faith, with that monistic immediacy the impulse to which and the sanction for which are from outside, from a carefully manipulated and sealed discourse. Of course, in distinguishing between the two, one may find it rewarding to relate them, which is what I have meant to do here. In doing so, I have suggested a helpful solution to that central and controlling problem of recent criticism that seeks to find the proper relation between poetry and beliefs.

Poetry, then, can produce this monistic experience of the symbol not because of an unfettered, immediate transfer of experience such as we saw Eastman speak of, but because of its willingness to construct itself as a totally enclosed set of mirrors that would seem to cut it off from that experience. With the un-self-conscious immediacy of primitive language experience lost to us, only a discourse that dedicates itself to disrupting the normal dualism which a culture finds in its Platonized discourse has a chance to force us to respond to it as its own entity. This becomes perhaps the most crucial justification of the contextualist approach to poetry, for only this approach can preserve poetry as our primary form of discourse and as the cultivated, self-conscious equivalent of our primary way of knowing (even if a more sophisticated —which is to say, a more mediate, dualistic—way of knowing would, properly, not admit it as knowledge at all). This approach comes yet another way at the primacy of poetry in constituting man's world for him. It thus supports Vivas' claim, discussed earlier, about the "insistent" priority of the role of poetry in creating a culture's self-awarenesses before "existent" propositional strategies ideologize, institutionalize, and devitalize them. In our humanity we must have the primitive grasp of these existential awarenesses—our sense of ourselves, our place and time—again and again, long after our language and our language psychology have lost the primitive immediacy needed to present them to us. It is poetry's character as effigy that gives them to us still.

It is for these reasons that, from the start, I have asserted that the poetic context has what, on the phenomenological level, seems to be a unique power of creativity, in contrast to other modes of discourse, however constitutive the neo-Kantian epistemology may see all language as being. Out of the death of animism in our symbols, now converted to the stale efficacy of signs, comes the self-conscious poetic context as the only agent that can force any magic—the magic of an indwelling creativity—into discourse.

But for all the power of effigy that a contextual poetry can establish, for all the conviction of its immanent here-ness, we have still theoretically to return this power to its culture; it is this culture's momentary vision that is the source of the total existential awareness poetry should give us, that allows its operation as window to be rendered as completely and as uniquely as is its operation as enclosed set of mirrors. We have seen earlier, in Spitzer's three criteria and in what I said of historicists like Auerbach or Pearce as I distinguished their ideas from a notion like Vivas' "insistence," that there is on the one hand the unique existential context of cultural forces and there is on the other hand the unique poetic context of the literary work; but, most problematically, there is the relation between the two, the extent to which and ways in which the latter may be said to reflect the former.

Given the aesthetic on one side and the existential on the other, what do we mean—when we speak of the poem as a reflection of the existential in the aesthetic mode—by that deceptive term "reflection," deceptive in that its elusive meaning gives us more confidence than we have theoretically earned? To what extent do we speak of the poem as the *bearer* of the vision of its culture's existential reality, to what extent as the *creator* of this vision (thus making it also its own aesthetic vision)? If the poem has its reality in the irreducible, untranslatable, aesthetic realm, then dare we merely take this word "reflection" as an elegant variation of the more candid term "imitation"? Despite its sealed context, the poem is seen as referring to, as imitating, existential forces that enter the work as its raw materials but that achieve their initial creation and definition in discourse only in and through poetry. This much I have claimed from the first in acknowledging that the work can be in a crucial sense imitative, if not in the sense normally intended by the mimetic tradition. But how can we know whether it is indeed imitative, that is, how can we measure its fidelity to existential forces, so long as these forces—as existential and thus as not yet institutionalized in propositions—have no other way of achieving discursive status as entities? Against what, then, can we check the "insistent" reality of the poem? For any attempt at a propositional translation that would institutionalize it is necessarily post-poetic and, in its reduced dimensions, can hardly be a measure of the authenticity of the poem.

So not only does the work begin in bit-by-bit imitation of identifiable elements in the culture that surrounds and nourishes it, but it also may end—as an integral poetic context that transmutes these elements—in imitation of existential forces external to it. But we cannot identify what the work ends by being an imitation *of,* since it must be the creator as well as the bearer of its vision so that only it can lead us to its object of imitation. It was with this claim in mind that I earlier insisted that, where the poem imitates "truly existential and pre-conceptual forces, one cannot know what was being imitated until after the poet has made it perceptible—which is to say, after he has created it to show what it was he imitated." We must theoretically earn our right to speak of this reflective (or imitative) relation between these two contexts, the poetic and the existential, to cross from one to the other, to move from the aesthetic to the thematic, without sacrificing the proper nature of either.

My definition of what I elsewhere have termed "thematics" indicates how central my claim of union between these two contexts must be: " . . . the study of the experiential tensions which, dramatically entangled in the literary work, become an existential reflection of that work's aesthetic complexity. Thematics thus conceived is as much beyond 'philosophy'— and in the same way beyond 'philosophy'—as, in pure poetics, an organic, contextually responsible form is beyond a logically consistent system."[8] And, in accordance with this definition and its use of that troublesome term "reflection," I

[8] *The Tragic Vision,* p. 242. A significant difference should be noted between my use of "thematics" and Frye's use of "thematic" (*Anatomy of Criticism,* pp. 52–55, 367). Frye opposes "thematic" to "fictional"; the former urges the primacy of thought rather than of plot or character (to use the Aristotelian terms Frye adapts for himself). For Frye, thematic interest is an interest in "the *point* of this story," an interest in the conceptual nature of its argument. Thus his "thematic" is clearly derived from our usual sense of the term *theme* (by which we really mean the series of propositions which we can extrapolate from the work's aesthetic totality), while I specifically distinguish my "thematics" from the commonplace notion of separable philosophic theme (*The Tragic Vision,* p. 241). For my "thematics" springs directly out of the work's "fictional" aspects (note the "dramatically entangled" in my definition) even as Frye's "thematic" is opposed to them. It is precisely this difference between the monistic or contextualist aesthetic and the dualistic or imitationist aesthetic that I have stressed from the beginning.

explored "aesthetic-formal" and "thematic-existential" motives in my first chapter, above, finding one to be the echo of the other. Still the question remains, the old cognitive question which even our newer formulations cannot evade or quite answer: how, without resorting to a form-content dichotomy, can we depend on the work's context to be an accurate "reflection" of those otherwise unavailable existential forces of the cultural context? One may grant the critic's aesthetic claim that objective judgment of poems is possible, and even necessary, since the critic must begin by establishing whether or not, or to what extent, the work before him is a mirrorized glass house before he can investigate its extraordinary claims to existential revelation. To make this decision is to make an aesthetic judgment. But how does the demonstration that the work is a mirrorized glass house ensure the accuracy of its historical and anthropological vision? How can the aesthetic judgment be shown to have such rare cognitive consequences? Through what coincidence is aesthetic complexity somehow the accurate "reflection" of existential complexity so that aesthetic soundness automatically, as it were, involves historic authenticity? Surely the rules of procedure and the criteria for judgment must be quite different for each of these. A weakness in the poetic structure, after all, is an aesthetic weakness, not an anthropological weakness. How can we relate it to the latter when it is so clearly the former? All this is to ask again, how do the enclosed mirrors convert to enchanted windows? As we have seen before, the theorist dares to make his task this difficult, not to give up on it, but to justify his invoking the miracle and his using the theoretical language at his disposal to make this miracle seem not altogether unreasonable.

Where I originally defined my sense of "thematics," I suggested that the notion of extremity, or literary casuistry, could be made to connect the aesthetic to the existential since it is a category that partakes of both realms: " . . . for the poet to formulate the extreme situation is indeed for him to play the casuist by purifying experience of the casual; . . . through the narrow intensity of *a fortiori* controls, the extreme situation can manage to account for the total breadth of experience, for all that is less committed and more compromising—and compromised. This is in effect what Henry James means in speaking of actual life that 'persistently blunders and deviates, loses herself in the sand,' in his complaints against the 'stupid work' of 'clumsy' raw experience which, unpurified, not merely militates against art but obfuscates its own meaning, leaving to art the role of mining this meaning anew. The extreme, then, is both more pure and more inclusive—pure in the adulterations it rejects and inclusive in the range of less complete experiences it illuminates even as it passes them by. Thus at once the rarity and the density, the order and the plenitude."[9]

Of course, these words most immediately apply to modern novels, and especially modern novels of the "tragic vision." Surely it is in these that extremity is obviously a central concern. The author plays the casuist, dedicated to extremity, by committing himself in the work absolutely to a reduction of one sort of experience to another, to a transfer of properties of one to those of another, a transfer to which every element in the work lends itself totally. Experience of a normal sort— messy, pre-poetic, of mixed and uncertain tendencies, veering in this direction and in that, impure in its continual compromise with the totality of definition—is viewed under the aspect of an extremely delimited sort of experience that threatens, momentarily, within its context, to reduce all experience to itself and to read life within its own awesome terms as unbearable and—to a common-sense reason that needs life as mixed—as irrational, even impossible.

Thus, in Mann's *Doctor Faustus*, for example, all forces lend themselves to reveal the generally accepted world of

[9] *The Tragic Vision*, p. 256.

artistic dedication and controlled artistic creativity exclusively under the aspect of the world of disease, to reveal the world of decent austerity and harsh asceticism exclusively under the aspect of the world of license. But the total transfer of properties, the total reduction, is deceptive. The terms I have used in my hasty oversimplification of these worlds should indicate that even as the extremes are poetically equated they remain polarized. In furnishing us a very paradigm of the functioning of extremity, Mann allows no mediation between extremes, but forces one to support the other, even to reflect the other, finally to become a mask for the other. Mann's extreme necessarily bears its opposite within itself by the very nature of its seemingly singleminded purity. The ill-defined, mixed components of the life he deals with follow the path of their most dangerous tendencies to extremes that are at once polar and reversible, opposed and identical. For the equation of the two worlds, the reduction of one to the other, becomes a substantive metaphor. As such it turns on itself, asserting for common sense the duality of its terms, the distinctness of their properties, even as it works the miracle of transubstantiation. Everything in the work—character, incident, language, style —contributes to the collapsing of the broad and mixed world to the narrow and pure one and thus to the creation of the work as a total metaphor, except that, even as the transfer becomes dramatically complete, the separateness of elements asserts itself to our rational, less totally committed selves.

It is in this sense that I see Mann's version of extremity as a paradigm that allows us to consider the poet's casuistry more broadly, so as to turn it into a generic literary strategy that can serve us with lyrics as well. To use another obvious example to which I have referred earlier, I can cite Donne's lovers in *The Canonization*, whose absorption by earthly love —which is shown in its normal state to be woefully mixed and incomplete in its nature—we are forced to view under the aspect of the total and unworldly dedication that earns sainthood. Everything in the poem, in the fullness of its contextual interrelations, works to bring off the equation, to complete the metaphor in its transfer of properties from tenor to vehicle (from earthly lovers to saints), even though the tenor and vehicle seem opposed to one another. Nevertheless this step-by-step extension of the metaphor carries along with it the covert guide of rationality that asserts the absurdity, even the speciousness, of this extension.[10] It is not that the identity produced by the metaphor is being denied, since such a denial would lead us outside the context and its mutually dependent terms, but that the miracle can be asserted as miracle only by continually recognizing its impossibility, by continually acknowledging the intransigence of the materials and oppositions being mastered, though they are never destroyed.

Such a miracle of substantive identity should of course not be viewed as a propositional truth claim (A is B) any more than it is a dramatic demonstration of a propositional moral claim (A ought to be B). With its context totally working to create it, it is rather a total and totally committed incarnation, an effigy of mixed and intransigent experience which has been substantively transferred into, or rendered within, an extreme, unmitigated reduction of one pure and narrow aspect to whose sway all cooperates or conspires in order to make the transfer complete—even as the miracle asserts itself as such by urging an awareness of its denial. Like Shakespeare's Phoenix and Turtle, like his mirror and window, like the *in* and the *through* of contextualism, but perhaps most like Clarissa's scissors which the baron manipulates in *The Rape of the Lock*,[11] the miraculous metaphor divides even while it joins.

In its simultaneous performing of its dividing and joining

[10] See *The New Apologists for Poetry*, pp. 13–18, for a detailed expansion of these claims about *The Canonization*.

[11] Indeed, like that miraculous poem itself, which creates its vision of the prosaic world of flesh and blood under the aspect of the airiness of the pure world of absolute play.

functions, its opening out and closing in functions, the dual nature of the extremity that leads to miracle—but a special sort of miracle at once assertive and denying—can correct an unfortunate over-emphasis that has for good reason bothered students of recent criticism. From Aristotle onward, critics, in insisting on the unity of the literary work, have insisted upon its convergent movement toward a unitary, sharply pointed conclusion and conclusive meaning. The *Poetics* traces, in the development of the literary work, the gradual, inevitable elimination of the multiple probabilities with which it began until, when the climax turns the complication into the denouement, only the one way that—though hidden to us and to the protagonist—has been inescapably there all along is left and is pursued to its end. It has been hard to improve upon this classic formulation in its convergent simplicity. Thus it could not help seeming dangerously perverse to find recent critics rather emphasizing almost exclusively the divergent meanings of literary works. While also insisting upon unity, they dwell upon the *organic* nature of that unity, upon the *variety* which is being unified. They celebrate the ambiguous instead of the unilinear, the unresolved tensions among centrifugal forces instead of the crowning assertion of the all-dominating centripetal force. At their more reckless moments they may seem to be claiming for the work no more narrowly unified a precision than that of a shotgun blast. And yet they have on the whole been persuasive about the many voices with which even an apparently simple poem may often speak. I am suggesting that literary extremity and its miracle, with the completeness of their absorption of alien, resistant, and incomplete materials together with the completeness of the unbridgeable separateness of these elements, can allow for the combined emphasis on the divergent and convergent natures of literary movement and meaning, the density and plenitude on the one side, the rarity and the order on the other. It can insist on the centrifugal thrust of a work only while placing its control within the pressing and uncompromising union of its finest and most centered point. The impossible combination of identity and polarity can make a total view of the object possible: the perspective is reduced to a single point even as, at the same time, the range of possibilities multiplies endlessly—thus the consequence of the object as both single substantive world and as bodiless reflection of multiple worlds beyond.

At this point we may wish to remember that even Frazer had effigies functioning both ways. Along with those magical effigies his 19th-century positivism deplores, in which the image is endowed with substance, he describes effigies in which the insubstantial sense of mere imitation is so strong that they are used *instead* of the real object of imitation in order to protect the substantial creature by providing this insubstantial substitute.[12] Nor, I think, does this occasional awareness of effigy as mere sign damage the conclusions I earlier tried to draw from the fully empowered effigy about the unitive language of primitive animism. On the contrary, I think it enforces them. The awareness of the bread figure as bread need not prevent the god from entering it. As Shakespeare so often shows us, there can be no miracle that does not insist on being had both ways, at once asserting itself as miracle and asserting its own impossibility (which proves it as nothing less than miracle) by showing our common sense its denial, at once demonstrating its substantive union and the unyielding matter of its separateness. For, as we have seen in Shakespeare's dealings with the marketplace, common-sense reason is both itself and its own parody. Which is why, as in *The Phoenix and Turtle* too, the poetic miracle, like eternity, can tease reason out of thought.

[12] See *The Golden Bough,* pp. 488–491, 494–499, 650, for descriptions of effigies endowed with substance, and pp. 491–493 for descriptions of effigies whose value is that they may serve *instead* of the substantial object of imitation.

III. THE POWER OF POETIC EFFIGY

In the lyric, in which the disciplines and the compression tighten the context most obviously, the total transfer, the visioning of one world under the aspect of another—its narrow, purified, extreme extension—may be followed immediately through the technical manipulation of metaphor, especially in the hands of a Donne or a Shakespeare, where its subtle development reaches the fullness of an earned conceit. This incarnating metaphor is again a total commitment to which every aspect of the context lends itself in order to close about the here-ness captured by effigy, even as its acknowledgment of miracle acknowledges also its absurdity and impossibility, denying its miracle only to maintain the need to assert it. As this total commitment, this metaphor keeps us still within the casuistic, the extreme creation of an equation that must be substantively, bodily made, in defiance of all other discourse and its logic. It does not, let me repeat, assert the equation as true but asserts it as miracle; that is, it does not assert it as true but asserts the need of our experience to be visioned this way if we are to order it, to understand it in its immediate purity of implication. It is a purity of implication which we never dare assert propositionally that our experience has, for it has so much else as well that would give any such assertion the lie, or more important, so much else that would allow other assertions to claim to be just as true; but we cannot afford *not* to see this experience as having become totally this vision. For it is this metaphor, this total substitution, that allows us to see what an historical moment, in the privacy of hidden, personal inwardness has, in its most daring creations, in the total metaphors of its single, reduced moments of vision, dared make of its world.

Out of these will proceed safer, more modified, more domesticated forms which can stereotype and institutionalize these perceptions so that they can enter the history of ideas, ideology, and formalized action. But the pure symbols remain at the base of our confrontation of experience, activating life in their more brute and more immediate way. Of this most primitive way we have never rid our aboriginal selves, even though—except for the self-consciousness of art—we have got rid of the unitive language we need to bring them in their pure state, via the extremities that at once polarize and equate, to the phenomenal level. Here, in the extremity of metaphor, in the totality of commitment to the purity of a single, reduced moment of vision, the two contexts—the existential context of cultural forces and the poetic context—collapse into one and the definition of "thematics" as their one common realm may be seen as theoretically earned.

We are left, then, to assert a double difference between the fully incarnating metaphor and lesser attempts at metaphor that fall short of the fully contextual poem, of the fully empowered effigy, as I have defined these. First, there is the difference with which I began: in the lesser attempt at metaphor there remains a duality between the tenor and vehicle, so that only a partial substitution of terms and properties has taken place and we are allowed to remain reasonably aware of the dissimilarities as well as the similarities between the elements of the would-be metaphor. As discourse it can be seen, as Tate some time ago told us, as an incomplete apology for a lack of science.[13] It may be that such an incomplete metaphor is originally representative of cultural forces that are pre-conceptually operative in our temperaments and are seeking monistic, incarnating expression; but so long as there is but a partial insistence on similarities, with the common-sense dissimilarities also acknowledged, then in this metaphor these forces have not yet achieved their discursive creation. In the fully incarnating metaphor, on the other hand, through the total dedication to and definition within the reduced and *a fortiori* aspect, unitive language is achieved for these forces. They are no

---

[13] "Three Types of Poetry," *On the Limits of Poetry*, p. 99: "For the apparent hostility of science to the allegorical entities is old age's preoccupation with the follies of its youth." See also p. 107.

longer left ungrown but develop into full symbols. The poetic context pushes them to their completion, which is to say to their extremity, finally transforming them by way of the miracle that produces the absolute equivalence of incarnation—that which our personal and cultural temperaments may hiddenly feel or have experienced but cannot otherwise express, given the Platonization of our discourse.

But now we are able to see a second difference join the first. The incomplete attempt at metaphor, having resisted absolute union by holding onto dissimilarities, must also in its rhetorical form remain reasonable and single-minded, respectful of the law of contradiction, the law of identity. This is to say that even if it were capable of total equation, despite reasonable demurrers—and it probably cannot be—still this equation would remain a point-by-point substitution and nothing more. Surely it would not be the sudden blooming that produces the miracle, so that the sense of the separateness of its elements would remain. On the other hand, the incarnating metaphor, in its total commitment to extremity and to identity in Mann's ambiguous sense, polarizes the very elements it identifies, and in the same act. Through its acknowledgment of the impossibility of the very movement it is dedicated to produce, it denies precisely, if often only implicitly, the miraculous equation it must make. This implicit denial permits it to urge its equation in the teeth of common sense, as it carries within its miraculous self the conviction of its own absurdity. This second difference, then, ends by seeming another way of describing the first difference, above, since only the total commitment to a context that, from the propositional viewpoint, seems self-contradictory, can produce the equation between identity and polarity. And to work in this way the context must be closed. Yet once closed, the context proceeds to create the very self-denial that its incarnation needs for us to capitalize the "I" to make it the Incarnation, the total em*body*ing of our world: for it reveals the miracle of what discourse can accomplish through the destruction of its normal, its reasonable, and, from the existential viewpoint, its bankrupt dimensions. It reproduces us at our pre-propositional, aboriginal levels, when we create our universe as an immediate universe of substance, as that "world's body" with which Ransom so properly concerned himself.

We are, of course, still in Shakespeare's world of love's unreasonable reason, with his *Sonnets* as its voice. They enunciate, in the daring movement to eschatology, the awareness of what the final extremity of love's devotion calls for, just as the total reduction of the practical world to the world of worms, of self-love to self-destruction, of business-like proficiency to mystic bafflement, enunciates the awareness of what the final extremity of the worldly alternative to love's devotion must lead to. Always there is the grudging battle with the way of the common-sense world, but as the poet reduces the latter he never neglects to give it its due, never bypasses its implied judgment of the extravagance of his extremity and its reductions. There could be no miracle in *The Phoenix and Turtle*, we must remember, unless reason itself was there to proclaim it—proclaiming with it, of course, its downright impossibility. But how else can one claim a miracle?[14] Nor, in Sonnets 30–31, could there be the literal and substantive growth of the present "thou" to the timeless "all they" without the surrounding futility of the world of finance, with all its precision and the discreteness of its sense of property. The world of finance remains to the end, its routine doggedness undercutting what transcends it and forcing us to remember the "thou" as only and uniquely "thou" even as the metaphorical structure of Sonnet 31 earns "thou" the right also to become "all they." Thus the Incarnation here seems

---

[14] Has not Spitzer in his tribute to what poetry makes of our old common words, has not Tate in his tribute to what the firm tension produced by the symbolic imagination makes of the "common thing," and have not others been telling us as much from the beginning of this essay?

indeed to have won its way to the capital "I," since, as I have suggested, in some ways it even approaches eschatology. And so it is, we have seen, with the *Sonnets* generally, at least within the metaphorical system I have provided for them here in viewing them as the corporate expression of love's faith.

So we have returned once more, as always, to the *Sonnets*. In treating them for themselves, I have found in them a key to the nature of metaphor, of poetry, and of poetics as well. For me they have been a microcosm that illuminates the macrocosm of poetry. Just as, taking the lead from Auerbach, I have used the typological instrument of the *figura* at crucial places throughout this work, so it should be clear that I have used the *Sonnets* themselves figurally, finding them to serve me as the typological *figura* of poetry at large and of modern poetics. I have tried to make clear both the prefiguring and the fulfillment. Thanks to the *Sonnets*, the substance of my own book becomes its method; for in it the *Sonnets* become a mirrow-window of and to themselves and my total subject. If I have at all succeeded in using them in this way, then this book itself becomes another tribute to their endless and ever-enlarging powers.

INDEX

Abrams, M. H., *The Mirror and the Lamp*, 3n
Adams, Hazard, "The Criteria of Criticism in Literature," 47n
allegory, religious, 8; as sign, 48–49
Arnold, Matthew, *Dover Beach*, 146
Aristotle, *Poetics*, 16, 17, 18, 20, 22, 196, 212
Auerbach, Erich, *Mimesis*, 11–12, 27, 54, 55–56, 116n, 175–76, 199n, 205, 218. *See also figura*

beliefs in poetry, 8–9, 12–14, 26, 28, 200–01, 202–04
Blake, William, 44, 46, 47
Böhme, Jakob, 32n
Brooks, Cleanth, 24, 27, 55, 56, 193n; *The Well Wrought Urn*, 193n; and W. K. Wimsatt, *Literary Criticism: A Short History*, 24n
Burckhardt, Sigurd, 14–16, 24, 27, 54, 63–64, 134n, 201; "The Poet as Fool and Priest," 14n, 63n; and R. H. Pearce, "Poetry, Language, and the Condition of Modern Man," 63

Cassirer, Ernst, 44, 53, 56–57
Cicero, 199
Coleridge, Samuel Taylor, 50
Contextualism, aesthetic monism of, 204–05; affirmation of miraculism, 66; alternatives to, 42–44, 48; as basis of modern criticism, 28; coordinated with new historicism, 58; criticism of, 36–37; definition of, 29; as distinct from myth criticism, 52–53; major contribution of,

41; Manichaean implications of, 19n; sign vs. symbol in, 30; and the *Sonnets*, 73–74, 201–03, 211, 213, 217–18; thematic dualism of, 19n, 25n
Cope, Jackson I., *The Metaphoric Structure of "Paradise Lost,"* 195n
Crane, R. S., "The Critical Monism of Cleanth Brooks," 35n
Croce, Benedetto, *Aesthetic*, 62n
Cunningham, J. V., *Tradition and Poetic Structure*, 165–66

Dante, *The Divine Comedy*, 8–13
Donne, John, 7, 15–16, 95, 109n, 158, 159, 163, 193, 210–11; *The Canonization*, 7, 95, 193, 210–11; *A Valediction Forbidding Mourning*, 15, 109n, 158, 159, 163

Eastman, Max, *The Literary Mind*, 34–36, 204
effigy, as monistic symbol, 6, 26, 193–199
Empson, William, 15, 134n
expressionism, as form of imitation, 41

Faustbook, 60, 62
figura (Auerbach), application to the *Sonnets*, 218; and double reality, 11–12, 199n; related to word "figure," 116n; and the typological view of history, 175
Foster, Richard, *The New Romantics: a Reappraisal of the New Criticism*, 43n
Frazer, Sir James George, *The Golden Bough*, 26, 194, 197n, 198–99, 200, 213

Frye, Northrop, 3n, 42–49, 51, 202, 207n; *The Anatomy of Criticism*, 42, 44, 46, 207n; "Myth, Fiction, and Displacement," 44n

Goethe, Johann Wolfgang, *Faust*, 62

Hausman, Carl R., "Art and Symbol," 30n
Hegel, Georg Wilhelm Friedrich, 18
Herrick, Robert, 63
Hobbes, Thomas, 194n
Hoffman, Frederick J., *The Mortal No: Death and the Modern Imagination*, 54
Honig, Edwin, *Dark Conceit: the Making of Allegory*, 48–49, 51
Hopkins, Gerard Manley, 63

imitation, as beginning of art, 26, 196; of existential forces, 206–07; in history of literary theory, 40–41; in Shakespeare's concept of art, 104
incarnation, as corporeality, 14; in new historicism, 64; as substantive body, 24; as substantive body in prose, 16–17; of the word in the *Sonnets*, 188–190; in the word, 15, 216–18

James, D. G., *Scepticism and Poetry*, 50
James, Henry, 209
Juan de la Cruz, 13, 32n

Kant, Immanuel, 57, 61
Krieger, Murray, "Contextualism was Ambitious," 40n; "The Dark Generations of *Richard III*," 136n, 176n; "*Dover Beach* and the Tragic Sense of Eternal Recurrence," 146n; "The 'Frail China Jar' and the Rude Hand of Chaos," 63n; *The New Apologists for Poetry*, 15n, 28, 34n, 50n, 52n, 187n, 211; review of R. Foster's *The New Romantics*, 43n; *The Tragic Vision*, 17n, 19n, 25n, 207n, 209n

Lawrence, D. H., 63
Lévy-Bruhl, Lucien, 25–26, 198
Lovejoy, A. O., 53

Mallarmé, Stéphane, 29
Manichaean, 19–21, 25, 38
Mann, Thomas, *Doctor Faustus*, 21, 62, 197, 209–10, 216
Marino, Giovanni Battista, 13n
Marlowe, Christopher, *Faustus*, 60–62
Marvell, Andrew, 13, 200; "Nymph Complaining for the Death of Her Fawn," 200
Melville, Herman, *Moby Dick*, 21
metaphor, incarnating vs. lesser, 215–17; the miracle in, 4–7; as poetics, 4; and religious allegory, 8–9
miraculism, of art, 22; as both unity and variety, 211–13; extension through *figura*, 12; extension through "Poetic Way," 10; in "law of participation," 25–26, 193–94, 198–99; in literature generally, 22–24; and metaphor, 7; poetic and religious, 9–14; and the *Sonnets*, 66–67; substantive powers of, 12, 13; and the substantive in recent criticism, 28, 200
Myth criticism, limitations of, 50–51, 53; as mysticism, 52; and mythic order of language, 44–48; as related to New Criticism, 49

New Criticism, 3, 37–39, 44, 48, 49, 51, 52n, 53, 62n. *See also* contextualism

new historicism, and corporeality, 64; definition of, 53; distinctions within, 58–66; as existential anthropology, 66; restrictions on expressive powers of poetry, 54–56

Nietzsche, Friedrich Wilhelm, 18, 23

Ong, Walter J., 195n

Panofsky, Erwin, *Meaning in the Visual Arts*, 54, 56–57

Pearce, Roy Harvey, 54–55, 63, 64, 205; *The Continuity of American Poetry*, 55n; "Historicism Once More," 55n; and S. Burckhardt, "Poetry, Language, and the Condition of Modern Man," 55n, 63

Plato, 20, 22, 83, 194

Pope, Alexander, 38, 63n, 211; *The Dunciad*, 38; *The Rape of the Lock*, 211

Ransom, John Crowe, *The World's Body*, 7–8, 9, 10, 11, 12, 13, 24, 27, 82n, 187–88, 194, 217

Richards, I. A., 34–36, 48; *Principles of Literary Criticism*, 34n; *Science and Poetry*, 34n

Shakespeare, William, 15, 27, 32, 63n, 66–67, 73–190, 193, 201–03, 211, 213, 217–18; *Henry IV*, 136, 140; *Measure for Measure*, 166; *The Phoenix and Turtle*, 80n, 150–54, 159, 160, 193, 211, 213, 217; *The Rape of Lucrece*, 85–86, 87; *Venus and Adonis*, 92–93, 158; Sonnets, *see* Index of Sonnets, p. 223

Shapiro, Karl, "A Farewell to Criticism," 31, 32n

Shelley, Percy Bysshe, 52

Sidney, Sir Philip, 203

sign, distinguished from symbol, 30–31; as referent in monistic claim, 193; and substantive oneness in the *Sonnets*, 202; and symbol in myth criticism, 48–49, 50–51

Sophocles, *Oedipus the King*, 19

Spenser, Edmund, 4n, 76–77, 78, 82, 83–85, 87, 90–91, 92; *Amoretti*, 76–77, 78, 83–85, 87, 92; *The Shepherd's Calendar*, 90–91

Spitzer, Leo, *Essays on English and American Literature*, 12–13, 27, 28, 31–32, 65–66, 200, 203, 205, 217n

Stevens, Wallace, 63

Sutton, Walter, 40n

symbol, *see* sign

Tate, Allen, 5, 7, 8–10, 11–12, 20, 24, 27, 194, 215, 217n; *The Man of Letters in the Modern World*, 5n, 9n; *On the Limits of Poetry*, 5n, 8n, 215n

Tennyson, Alfred, Lord, *Tithonus*, 88

tension, and catharsis, 18, 20, 23–24; in metaphor, 5–6; in modern literature, 20–23

thematics, aesthetic-formal motive of, 19–22, 208; definition of, 207; in existential and poetic contexts, 207–08, 215; thematic-existential motive of, 19–22, 208

tragic vision, extremity in, 18–19, 23, 208–11; as "insistential," 63; and substantive body in prose, 17–22

Tuve, Rosemund, 194n

Vivas, Eliseo, 59–63, 196n, 205; *Creation and Discovery*, 59n, 196n; *D. H. Lawrence: the Failure and Triumph of Art*, 59n; "The Object of the Poem," 59; "A Semantic for Humanists," 50n

Wheelwright, Philip, *The Burning Fountain*, 25–26, 49–52, 57, 193–95, 197n, 200, 204

Williams, Charles, 9

Wimsatt, W. K., 24, 25n, 27; and C. Brooks, *Literary Criticism: A Short History*, 24n; "Poetic Tension: A Summary," 24n

Winters, Yvor, 6n

Wordsworth, William, 29

Yeats, William Butler, 44, 47, 73; *A Vision*, 73

INDEX OF SONNETS

Sonnet	Quoted on	Discussed on
1	93–94	88, 89, 94–96, 107–08, 117, 118, 128;
2	—	118n;
3	86–87	87–90, 92, 93, 96, 104, 165, 186;
4	94	89, 94–95, 108–09, 139, 180, 188;
5	111–12	88, 112–15;
6	112	95, 111, 116–17, 128, 174–75;
9	110	95, 109–11, 188;
12	97	88, 97–100;
13	108n	108n;
15	100–01	102–03, 107;
16	101	102–05, 107;
17	101–02	102, 104–07;
18	—	106n;
19	—	105n, 106n;
22	81n	81n;
23	75, 77	75–79, 82;
24	80	80–82, 165;
30	179	180–83, 184, 185, 186, 203, 217;
31	179–80	183–86, 203, 217;
33	—	131n, 135, 155, 157;
34	—	155–57;
35	156–57	157–58;
36	157	158, 159–60;
37	160, 161	159, 160–62, 164, 165, 177;
38	—	162;
39	162–63	159, 162–63, 164;
44	167	167–68;
45	167	167–68;
53	177	161n, 177–78, 186;
55	—	148n;
60	99	98–99, 125, 147n;
62	163–64	164;
63	—	125;
64	144	99n, 144–46, 168–70, 172;
65	170	144n, 146, 168, 170–72;
66	—	136n;
67	137	136n, 137–39, 154n, 164, 177;
68	137–38	137–39, 154n, 164, 177;
71	119	120–21, 125, 145n, 148, 154, 166, 180;
72	119	120–22, 125, 129, 166;
73	98–99	98, 123;
74	123	123–25, 149, 179, 180, 184;
76	189	189–90;

INDEX OF SONNETS

Sonnet	Quoted on	Discussed on	Sonnet	Quoted on	Discussed on
86	—	104n;	116	146–47	125, 146–50, 182;
87	133	131n, 133–37, 155, 166, 179, 180;	123	—	125;
			124	140	125, 140–44, 145, 146, 148, 149n;
96	—	160n;			
106	173	173–77, 186;	126	—	125;
113	129	129–30, 132, 178;	130	—	78n;
			136	—	151;
114	130–31	129, 130–33, 135, 155;	140	—	136n;
			144	—	128;
			146	125–26	124, 125–29